Face to Face
with a
Holy God

KAY ARTHUR
PETE De LACY

HARVEST HOUSE PUBLISHERS
EUGENE, OREGON

Bobbie Quigly

Chris Bunch &
Burris
Kia Dark

All Scripture references are taken from the New American Standard Bible®, © 1960, 1962, 1963, 1968, 1971, 1972, 1973, 1975, 1977, 1995 by The Lockman Foundation. Used by permission. (www.Lockman.org)

Cover by Koechel Peterson & Associates, Inc., Minneapolis, Minnesota

FACE-TO-FACE WITH A HOLY GOD
Copyright © 2008 by Precept Ministries International
Published by Harvest House Publishers
Eugene, Oregon 97402
www.harvesthousepublishers.com

Library of Congress Cataloging-in-Publication Data
Arthur, Kay, 1933-
Face-to-face with a Holy God/ Kay Arthur and Pete De Lacy.
    p. cm.—
ISBN 978-0-7369-2305-7 (pbk.)
1. Bible. O.T. Isaiah—Study and teaching. I. DeLacy, Pete. II. Title.
BS1515.55.A78 2008
224'.10071—dc22

                                                                          2008002113

Printed in the United States of America

16 17 18 19 20 / BP-SK / 14 13 12 11 10 9 8 7

CONTENTS

How to Get Started...

Reading directions is sometimes difficult and hardly ever enjoyable! Most often you just want to get started. Only if all else fails will you read the instructions. We understand, but please don't approach this study that way. These brief instructions are a vital part of getting started on the right foot! These few pages will help you immensely.

FIRST

As you study Isaiah, you will need four things in addition to this book:

1. A Bible that you are willing to mark in. The marking is essential. An ideal Bible for this purpose is *The New Inductive Study Bible (NISB)*. The *NISB* is in a single-column text format with large, easy-to-read type, which is ideal for marking. The margins of the text are wide and blank for note taking.

The *NISB* also has instructions for studying each book of the Bible, but it does not contain any commentary on the text, nor is it compiled from any theological stance. Its purpose is to teach you how to discern truth for yourself through the inductive method of study. (The various charts and maps that you will find in this study guide are taken from the *NISB*.)

Whichever Bible you use, just know you will need to mark in it, which brings us to the second item you will need...

2. A fine-point, four-color ballpoint pen or various colored fine-point pens that you can use to write in your Bible. Office supply stores should have those.

3. Colored pencils or an eight-color leaded Pentel pencil.

4. A composition book or a notebook for working on your assignments or recording your insights.

SECOND

1. As you study Isaiah, you will be given specific instructions for each day's study. These should take you between 20 and 30 minutes a day, but if you spend more time than this, you will increase your intimacy with the Word of God and the God of the Word.

If you are doing this study in a class and you find the lessons too heavy, simply do what you can. To do a little is better than to do nothing. Don't be an all-or-nothing person when it comes to Bible study.

Remember, anytime you get into the Word of God, you enter into more intensive warfare with the devil (our enemy). Why? Every piece of the Christian's armor is related to the Word of God. And our one and only offensive weapon is the sword of the Spirit, which is the Word of God. The enemy wants you to have a dull sword. Don't cooperate! You don't have to!

2. As you read each chapter, train yourself to ask the "5 W's and an H": who, what, when, where, why, and how. Asking questions like these helps you see exactly what the Word of God is saying. When you interrogate the text with the 5 W's and an H, you ask questions like these:

a. **What** is the chapter about?

b. **Who** are the main characters?

c. **When** does this event or teaching take place?

d. **Where** does this happen?

e. **Why** is this being done or said?

f. **How** did it happen?

3. Locations are important in many books of the Bible, so marking references to these in a distinguishable way will be helpful to you. I simply underline every reference to a location in green (grass and trees are green!) using my four-color ballpoint pen. A map is included on page 123 in this study so you can look up the locations.

4. References to time are also very important and should be marked in an easily recognizable way in your Bible. I mark them by putting a clock like this ⏰ in the margin of my Bible beside the verse where the phrase occurs. You may want to underline or color the references to time in one specific color.

5. You will be given certain key words to mark throughout this study. This is the purpose of the colored pencils and the colored pens. If you will develop the habit of marking your Bible in this way, you will find it will make a significant difference in the effectiveness of your study and in how much you remember.

A **key word** is an important word that the author uses repeatedly in order to convey his message to his readers. Certain key words will show up throughout Isaiah; others will be concentrated in a specific chapter. When you mark a key word, you should also mark its synonyms (words that mean the same thing in the context) and any pronouns (*he, his, she, her, it, we, they, us, our, you, their, them*) in the same way you have marked the key word. Also, mark each word the same way in all of its forms (such as *judge, judgment,* and *judging*). We will give you a few suggestions for ways to mark key words in your daily assignments.

You can use colors or symbols or a combination of colors and symbols to mark words for easy identification. However, colors are easier to distinguish than symbols. When we use symbols, we keep them very simple. For example, you could draw the outline of a book over *word* like this: and shade it yellow.

When marking key words, mark them in a way that is easy for you to remember.

If you devise a color-coding system for marking key words throughout your Bible, then when you look at the pages of your Bible, you will see instantly where a key word is used. You might want to make yourself a bookmark listing the words you mark along with their colors and/or symbols.

6. An ISAIAH AT A GLANCE chart is included on pages 121 and 122. As you complete your study of a chapter, record the main theme of that chapter under the appropriate chapter number. The main theme of a chapter is what the chapter deals with the most. It may be a particular subject or teaching.

If you fill out the ISAIAH AT A GLANCE chart as you progress through the study, you will have a synopsis of Isaiah when you are finished. If you have a *New Inductive Study Bible,* you will find the same chart in your Bible (pages 1193 and 1194). If you record your themes there, you will have them for a ready reference.

7. Always begin your study with prayer. As you do your part to handle the Word of God accurately, you must remember that the Bible is a divinely inspired book. The words that you are reading are truth, given to you by God so you can know Him and His ways more intimately. These truths are divinely revealed.

> For to us God revealed them through the
> Spirit; for the Spirit searches all things, even the

depths of God. For who among men knows the
thoughts of a man except the spirit of the man
which is in him? Even so the thoughts of God
no one knows except the Spirit of God (1 Corinthians 2:10-11).

Therefore ask God to reveal His truth to you as He leads
and guides you into all truth. He will if you will ask.

8. Each day when you finish your lesson, meditate on
what you saw. Ask your heavenly Father how you should
live in light of the truths you have just studied. At times,
depending on how God has spoken to you through His
Word, you might even want to write LFL ("Lessons for Life")
in the margin of your Bible and then, as briefly as possible,
record the lesson for life that you want to remember.

THIRD

This study is set up so that you have an assignment for
every day of the week—so that you are in the Word daily.
If you work through your study in this way, you will find
it more profitable than doing a week's study in one sitting.
Pacing yourself this way allows time for thinking through
what you learn on a daily basis!

The seventh day of each week differs from the other six
days. The seventh day is designed to aid group discussion;
however, it's also profitable if you are studying this book
individually.

The "seventh" day is whatever day in the week you choose
to finish your week's study. On this day, you will find a verse
or two for you to memorize and STORE IN YOUR HEART. Then
there is a passage to READ AND DISCUSS. This will help you
focus on a major truth or major truths covered in your study
that week.

To assist those using the material in a Sunday school class

or a group Bible study, there are QUESTIONS FOR DISCUSSION OR INDIVIDUAL STUDY. Even if you are not doing this study with anyone else, answering these questions would be good for you.

If you are in a group, be sure every member of the class, including the teacher, supports his or her answers and insights from the Bible text itself. Then you will be handling the Word of God accurately. As you learn to see what the text says and compare Scripture with Scripture, the Bible explains itself.

Always examine your insights by carefully observing the text to see what it *says*. Then, before you decide what the passage of Scripture *means,* make sure that you interpret it in the light of its context. Scripture will never contradict Scripture. If it ever seems to contradict the rest of the Word of God, you can be certain that something is being taken out of context. If you come to a passage that is difficult to understand, reserve your interpretations for a time when you can study the passage in greater depth.

The purpose of the THOUGHT FOR THE WEEK is to share with you what we consider to be an important element in your week of study. We have included it for your evaluation and, hopefully, for your edification. This section will help you see how to walk in light of what you learned.

Books in the New Inductive Study Series are survey courses. If you want to do a more in-depth study of a particular book of the Bible, we suggest you do a Precept Upon Precept Bible study course on that book. You may obtain more information on these courses by contacting Precept Ministries International at 800-763-8280, visiting our website at www.precept.org, or filling out and mailing the response card in the back of this book.

INTRODUCTION
TO ISAIAH

∽∾∽∾∽

After Solomon died, the kingdom of Israel was torn in two, and two new kingdoms formed. The northern kingdom, known thereafter as Israel, eventually had its capital in the city of Samaria. The southern kingdom was known as Judah, with its capital in Jerusalem.

Judah had only two tribes, Judah and Benjamin, and Israel had ten. Judah had a temple in Jerusalem, which housed the traditional worship system that began at Mount Sinai. The Levites and the Aaronic priesthood served in Jerusalem. In the north, Israel developed a new priesthood and a new worship system. Israel worshipped two golden calves—one in Bethel and one in Dan.

The two kingdoms were almost always at war. Israel declined under a succession of 17 idolatrous kings until the last of the kingdom was taken captive to Assyria in 722 BC. The southern kingdom was not much better. There were bright spots among the kings, a few revivals and returns to right worship, but idolatry never was eradicated, and God sent messenger after messenger, prophet after prophet.

Isaiah was one of those prophets. As you read, you'll

see when he prophesied by the names of the kings of Judah during his ministry. And as you read, you'll see why God sent him. The question for us to answer is, how does the message of Isaiah apply to us today? If we don't see the relevance, our study is interesting but of no value. So look for the message for you. See what you learn about God—His character and His ways. See what you learn about what He wants from those He loves, from His children. If you have believed the gospel of Jesus Christ, you are God's child, and this is an opportunity for you to listen to your Father.

The Lord Contends with His People

❧❧❧❧

God speaks to man through His Word, the Bible. But do we listen? Do we read it and obey it? God spoke to Israel through His holy prophets, and many of their words are included in the Bible. But Israel often had a problem obeying God, and they faced the consequences.

DAY ONE

As you read any book of the Bible, you'll see the author emphasize subjects by repeating key words and phrases. Since you'll be marking many of these words and phrases throughout Isaiah, a good technique is to record them and how you plan to mark them on a 3 x 5 card and use this as a bookmark. Doing this as you go from chapter to chapter will help you mark consistently and save time.

Now read through Isaiah 1 and mark every reference to *Israel, Lord, word,* and *sin.* You may want to mark *word* yellow and/or perhaps with the symbol of a book, like this: 📖 . Mark *Lord* with a purple triangle shaded yellow, *Israel* with

13

blue, and *sin* brown. Also double underline in green any geographical references, and underline the names of any kings.

Think about what you've marked. Why is God sending this message? What is the problem in Judah and Jerusalem? What will God do? Is there any hope for the people?

Now determine what this chapter is about and record a theme for the chapter ISAIAH AT A GLANCE on page 121.

DAY TWO

Don't forget to begin your study time with prayer. Remember, you have access to the Author, and He truly wants you to know, understand, and live by every word that comes from His mouth.

Take a moment to look at the chart on page 123 to see a timeline of kings and prophets. This will help you understand the historical context of Isaiah's life and writings.

Read 2 Kings 14:17–15:38 and 2 Chronicles 26:1–27:2 for insights on Uzziah (also called Azariah.)

Reviewing Israel's relationship to God will also be helpful, so read the following and consider why God can bring a "lawsuit" against Israel:

Exodus 24:1-8

Deuteronomy 28:1-20,45

Deuteronomy 30:1-5

DAY THREE

Today read Isaiah 2 and make sure to mark references to

time with a clock as we mentioned in "How to Get Started." However, mark *in the last days* differently from other time references.

Nations is a good word to mark throughout the Old Testament. Color it green and underline it with brown. Mark *proud*[1] with an arrow pointing up and *humble*[2] with an arrow pointing down. The Hebrew word translated *proud* literally means lifted up, and *humble* is the opposite of proud. Also mark *idols* and any synonyms for these key words.

Thinking about Isaiah 1 together with Isaiah 2, what does the future hold for Judah and Jerusalem? Is it good or bad?

Read Micah 4:1-3 and compare it to Isaiah 2:1-4. What do they have in common?

What about the proud? What's in store for them? What application can you make for your life? We can easily view Israel or Judah with disdain—judging them for their idolatry, pride, and wealth—and forget that God preserved these Old Testament examples for our instruction, upon whom the ends of the ages has come (Romans 15:4; 1 Corinthians 10:11).

God calls the house of Jacob to "walk in the light of the LORD." Does He expect any less from those in the New Covenant of grace? What about us? Are we walking in the light of the Lord or in the pride of life?

Think on these things and then record a theme for Isaiah 2 on ISAIAH AT A GLANCE.

DAYS FOUR & FIVE

Today read Isaiah 3 and 4 and mark the key words on your bookmark. Also mark *judge* (*judgment*), *wicked,* and *righteous,* and add these to your bookmark.

Make note of contrasts in these chapters. What is being

contrasted? How are those things different? You can find some contrasts by locating the word *instead.*

Mark any time references as you have before.

What is God going to do to Judah and Jerusalem and why? Is this consistent with Isaiah 1 and 2? Do you see anything new here? Who specifically is being held accountable in Isaiah 3?

What do the women mentioned in Isaiah 3 remind us about our own lives?

Do these chapters contain any hope? Why and how is it given? How does this compare with the hope in chapters 1 and 2?

Finally, record themes for Isaiah 3 and 4 on ISAIAH AT A GLANCE.

DAY SIX

Now we come to Isaiah 5—an incredible chapter. Read it, and in addition to the words on your bookmark, mark *people, exile,*[3] and *anger.*

Compare Hosea 4:1-6 with Isaiah 5:13. What is similar?

Are there any similarities between God's people in Isaiah's day and those who claim to know God today? Think of some examples. What effect should Isaiah's words have had on the people of his day? What effect do you think they would have today on the church? Do you hear messages like this very often today?

You might also have noticed the repetition of *woe* in Isaiah 5. What does this word draw attention to?

How is God going to bring judgment on Judah?

Don't forget to record a theme for Isaiah 5 on ISAIAH AT A GLANCE.

[handwritten margin notes at top: "...ons harsh but not loving but let people continue in sin He had been longsuffering"]

~~~~
## DAY SEVEN
~~~~

Store in your heart: Isaiah 1:18

Read and discuss: Isaiah 1:1-4,10-20; 2:1-4,12-18; 3:11-15; 4:1-6; 5:26-30

QUESTIONS FOR DISCUSSION OR INDIVIDUAL STUDY

[handwritten margin note: "What is world like"]

∾ Discuss the setting of Isaiah 1–5. What kings are reigning, and what do you know about the history of Judah?

[handwritten margin note: "ch 2. Day of reckoning"]

∾ What do you know about the relationship between God and the nation of Israel from Exodus and Deuteronomy?

∾ How does this relate to the message of Isaiah 1–5?

∾ What is the general message of Isaiah 5? What is the problem in Israel?

∾ What message of hope is given in these chapters?

∾ What application can you make to your own life? Are you a child of God? What is your response to God's forgiveness?

∾ How does this week's study motivate you to share what you learned with others?

THOUGHT FOR THE WEEK

"The LORD arises to contend, and stands to judge the people," Isaiah tells us in chapter 3, verse 13. His anger has burned against His people, and He has stretched out His hand against them and struck them down. For all this His anger is not spent; His hand is still stretched out.

What shall we make of such hostile words? What is the relationship between God and Israel? Chapter 1 gives us a description:

> Verse 2: Sons I have reared and brought up,
> But they have revolted against Me.

> Verse 3: An ox knows its owner,
> And a donkey its master's manger
> But Israel does not know,
> My people do not understand...

> Verse 4: Sons who act corruptly!
> They have abandoned the LORD,
> They have despised the Holy One of Israel,
> They have turned away from Him.

These give us some clues to the relationship. Verse 2 tells us about a father-son relationship. Verse 3 tells us about a master-servant relationship. Verse 4 tells us about both father-son and God-people relationships.

In Exodus 4:22-23, when God was sending Moses to Egypt to bring His people out of slavery, He told Moses to say to Pharaoh, "Israel is My son, My firstborn...Let My son go that he may serve Me." So we see God acknowledging Israel as His son. Isaiah, Jeremiah, Ezekiel, and Hosea all pick up this theme.

Exodus 34:23 introduces us to God as *Adonai,* the "Lord GOD, the God of Israel." Before that, the word *Adonai* is mostly translated as *master* and used of men. In Isaiah 5, Isaiah uses a metaphor of the vineyard and the owner. As Master, the owner of the vineyard, God expects good fruit.

We know from Exodus and Deuteronomy that Israel

entered into a covenant with God at Mount Sinai to be His people, and He would be their God. Deuteronomy 26:17-19, for example, establishes this relationship:

> You have today declared the LORD to be your God, and that you would walk in His ways and keep His statutes, His commandments and His ordinances, and listen to His voice. The LORD has today declared you to be His people, a treasured possession, as He promised you, and that you should keep all His commandments; and that He will set you high above all nations which He has made, for praise, fame, and honor; and that you shall be a consecrated people to the LORD your God, as He has spoken.

So what does God, this God who is Father and Master, expect from Israel?

> All the commandments that I am commanding you today you shall be careful to do, that you may live and multiply, and go in and possess the land which the LORD swore to give to your forefathers. You shall remember all the way which the LORD your God has led you in the wilderness these forty years, that He might humble you, testing you, to know what was in your heart, whether you would keep His commandments or not (Deuteronomy 8:1-2).

Notice what God said about obedience and humility. Deuteronomy 8:19 adds that if Israel ever forgets God and serves and worships other gods, they will surely perish because they would not listen to the Lord their God. And in Isaiah, we find Israel in exactly that situation. They have gone after other gods, to bow down and worship them, to serve them. So based on the relationship established in Exodus and Deuteronomy, God, the one who made the covenant, laid out clearly for His partner, Israel, what to expect if they broke the rules.

God, the Holy One of Israel, expects holy behavior from His sons, His children, His servants, His covenant partners. First Peter 1:14-16 quotes Leviticus 11:45: "You shall be holy, for I am holy." This is the standard to which God holds His people accountable. Because He is Holy, He can judge their holiness by His standard. And thus He has the right to judge righteously, as any father or master would.

So we know God has the authority to hold Israel accountable. This is the basis of the case He brings against Judah and Jerusalem in Isaiah. Remember, Judah and Jerusalem are simply what's left in the land of Israel. Judah is the southern kingdom, and Jerusalem is its capital.

Now, how does any of this relate to you and me? Is there any parallel to our situation as the church?

In the Sermon on the Mount, Jesus tells His listeners that they have a Father in heaven. The Gospels echo this term throughout because Jesus' audience in His earthly ministry was Jewish. But the term is clearly expanded to include the Gentiles.

According to John 1:12, we have the same God and Father that Israel does if we have believed in Jesus. And we have fellowship with Him.

The New Testament contains literally hundreds of references to Jesus as Lord, but perhaps none is better or more famous than Revelation 19:16: He is the "King of kings, and Lord of lords."

When God is done judging, purging, and restoring holiness, what will things be like? What can give New Testament believers motivation and hope as we consider the results of judgment?

We have the hope of resurrection, the hope of a new body, the hope of eternal life, the hope of reward, the hope of the return of Jesus to rule and reign, the hope of a new heaven and a new earth, and the hope of just judgment of the living and the dead.

HERE I AM, SEND ME

If God called us, would we hear His voice? Would we recognize it among all the other voices that call to us from every direction with every offer? And if we heard it, how would we respond? Would we be like Isaiah?

DAY ONE

Even if you've never studied the book of Isaiah or been in a church that taught it expositionally, you have probably heard a message based on chapter 6. If you've read through the Gospels or Acts, you've read a quote from this chapter. We need to understand and experience its place, content, and interpretation.

Read Isaiah 6:1 and mark the time reference. How does this compare with Isaiah 1:1? This new time marker means that the first five chapters were essentially one message, and now chapter 6 starts a new message.

Now read Isaiah 6, marking the key words on your bookmark. Add *holy, seeing,* and *hearing.* You could mark *seeing* with a pair of eyes and *hearing* with an ear.

23

Now let's look at the message. What did Isaiah see and hear? The Hebrew word translated *seraphim* means burning ones. May your heart burn within you in a purifying way as you study.

What was Isaiah's response? How did his response to God's holiness differ from King Uzziah's, which we saw in day 2 last week?

How does God respond to Isaiah?

What was Isaiah called to do? How would Israel respond to his message?

Now for some application. How important is it for people to see their sin? Have you seen yours? How is iniquity taken away and sin forgiven? Has yours been forgiven? How did you respond to God when He forgave you? How are you living today?

DAY TWO

Isaiah 6:9-10 are quoted in the New Testament more often than any other Old Testament verses. Read the following:

Matthew 13:13-17

Mark 4:10-12

Luke 8:9-10

John 12:37-41

Acts 28:23-29

What general truth can you discern from these verses?

Isaiah's call, Isaiah 6:9-12, could have been depressing for Isaiah except for Isaiah 6:13. How does this bring hope?

Read Matthew 7:13-14. What parallel to Isaiah 6:13 do you see?

Finally, thinking about all you have seen yesterday and today, what's the main subject of this chapter? Write this out as a theme for Isaiah 6 and record it on ISAIAH AT A GLANCE on page 121.

DAY THREE

The events of more than two and a half millennia ago that we're about to study can significantly shape the way we live. Then as now, the people of God were living in a culture that increasingly preferred darkness to light because their deeds were evil (John 3:19).

Many Christians are not familiar with the times and people of Isaiah 7–9. So how do we decipher its message and grasp its wisdom? If you understand this, you'll be instructed, find encouragement and hope, and persevere (Romans 15:4).

Read Isaiah 7 and mark time references, geographical locations, and the key words on your bookmark. Mark the following, but add only *Assyria* to your bookmark: *sign(s)*, *Assyria*, *Immanuel*, and *child*.[4]

What did you learn from marking *sign*, *Immanuel*, and *child*?

Now let's pause for some application. Let's examine our hearts in the light of Ahaz's refusal to ask for a significant sign God invited him to ask for. The sign would have given him light (proof), but what did Ahaz (from the house of David and therefore a beneficiary of the Davidic covenant) refuse to do? He refused to come to the light! Was it because he already had a plan, a solution? Yes, he did: He would depend on Assyria rather than depending on God (2 Kings 16:7; 2 Chronicles 28:16).

Finally, determine a theme for Isaiah 7 and record it on ISAIAH AT A GLANCE.

DAY FOUR

The saga continues. Ahaz may not listen, but Isaiah will. Read Isaiah 8:1–9:7. Mark the words on your bookmark, and include the *Lord said (spoke)*, *Maher-shalal-hash-baz*, *people*,[5] *God with us* (mark this as you marked *Immanuel* in Isaiah 7), *signs*, and *child*. Mark these last two as you did in Isaiah 7.

How does Isaiah 9:1-7 fit with Isaiah 8?

DAY FIVE

Now, considering Isaiah 8:1–9:7 as a unit, what is the first thing Isaiah is told to do, and who are the witnesses?

How long does it take for a child to learn to say "my father" or "my mother"? Why is this significant?

What picture does God give in 8:5-8? Where did Isaiah first address Ahaz?

Shiloah's waters are in Jerusalem, where God has put His name. What are the people turning to?

Read John 7:37-38. Who sustains us and satisfies our thirst?

Read Isaiah 8:9-15 again. Who is in charge, and what is Isaiah to do? Whom are the people to fear, and what will the child become?

"A stone to strike and a rock to stumble over"—do these words ring a bell? Read Romans 9:33 and 1 Peter 2:7-8. How do these relate to Isaiah 8:14-15? What do you see?

Isn't this awesome? God tucks prophetic jewels of truth in His words to Israel in this moment of their history, and then He lays them out before our eyes in all their glory thousands of years later!

DAY SIX

For our last day of study this week, we'll look at the references you marked to the *child* in Isaiah 7 and 9. List in two columns in your notebook what you observed about the child in Isaiah 7:14 and 9:6-7.

Now compare Isaiah 7:14 with Matthew 1:18-23. What do you see?

Compare Isaiah 9:6-7 with Luke 1:26-33; John 1:1,14; and Romans 1:3-4.

Make three columns in your notebook and list what you see about the child in Luke 1:26-33, the Word in John 1:1,14, and the Son in Romans 1:3-4.

Now compare Isaiah 9:1-2 with Matthew 4:12-16. Also read 2 Kings 15:29 and note what land was first captured, which people the Assyrians took into captivity, and under whose reign.

Prophecy can have both near fulfillment (close to the prophet's times) and far fulfillment (much later), so how would you interpret Isaiah 7:14 and 9:6-7?

Record a theme for Isaiah 8 on ISAIAH AT A GLANCE.

DAY SEVEN

 Store in your heart: Isaiah 7:14 and 9:6-7
Read and discuss: Isaiah 6; 7:10-17; 8:19–9:7

QUESTIONS FOR DISCUSSION OR INDIVIDUAL STUDY

∾ Describe the vision Isaiah had of the Lord.

∾ What was his reaction?

◌ Do you see yourself as Isaiah did? Why?

◌ What was God's call on Isaiah, and what was his reaction?

◌ Have you heard a call on your life from God? Share that call and your response.

◌ Illustrate from Isaiah how God's call can be difficult, and discuss how this relates to your situation.

◌ What did you learn about the virgin and child in Isaiah 7? What is the significance of this child?

◌ How does the child in Isaiah 7:14 relate to Isaiah 9:6-7?

◌ How does the contrast between the end of Isaiah 8 and the beginning of Isaiah 9 relate to the child?

THOUGHT FOR THE WEEK

Do we listen to God? When we listen, do we really hear? And when we hear, how do we respond? Isaiah was confronted with a vision of the holiness of God and heard the cry of the seraphim: "Holy, Holy, Holy is the LORD of Hosts, the whole earth is full of His glory." Isaiah listened and heard. His response was to recognize his own sinfulness. Then God called to him, and he responded, "Here am I. Send me!"

God calls to us today the same way. If we spend time in God's Word, especially the Old Testament, we see His holiness. The question is, will we recognize our own sin? Remember, even though we have believed the gospel and been cleansed of sin and forgiven, we're not without sin. First John 1:8-10 tells us that if we say we have no sin, we deceive ourselves, and the truth is not in us. If we say we have not sinned, we make God a liar. The proper response to sin is to confess it; then God will cleanse us and forgive it.

Often today we hear messages that emphasize an intimate friendship with God. Less often do we hear messages about the holiness and glory of God. Yet the glory of God was a key concept in the Old Testament, and certainly in Isaiah 6.

When the children of Israel came out of Egypt and wandered in the wilderness, the glory of God went before them in a pillar of fire by night and a pillar of cloud by day. At the crossing of the Red Sea, the glory of the Lord was Israel's rear guard against Pharaoh's army until they were safely across the dry land.

When God met them at Mount Sinai, His glory hovered over the mountain, appearing to Israel as fire, cloud, and thunder. When the tabernacle was erected, the glory of God filled it, and the priests were not even able to minister. When Solomon dedicated the temple he built in Jerusalem, just as when the tabernacle was dedicated, the glory of God filled the temple, and again the priests could not stand to minister.

Then in Ezekiel, during the time of the Babylonian captivity of Judah, the glory of God left the temple. Ezekiel's vision showed the glory rising up, moving east, and leaving the temple and then the city of Jerusalem.

The glory of the Lord did not return to that temple after the captivity. When the remnant returned and rebuilt the temple, the glory of God did not enter the temple again for more than 500 years. And then Mary and Joseph brought the baby Jesus into the temple for His dedication as required by the law. The prophet Simeon saw the baby and declared that now he had seen the glory of Israel.

The glory of God had returned in the person of Jesus. Jesus personified for us the holiness of God. He was conceived of the Holy Spirit, not the seed of Adam, and was without sin. He lived a perfectly obedient and sinless life, showing us what complete obedience to the Father looks like.

He spoke only what the Father told Him and did what the Father showed Him.

The writer of Hebrews tells us that Jesus is the radiance of God's glory and the exact representation of His nature. According to the Gospel of John, Jesus said those who see Him see the Father.

So today, we who believe the gospel, who encounter Jesus, see the glory of the Lord. But what is our response? Do we fall on our faces before God? Do we declare that we have unclean lips? Do we see the need to be cleansed of our sin? Do we really see the holiness of God?

And most of all, do we respond to God's call to us, saying "Here am I. Send me!" Are we willing to go and proclaim the message of salvation to a lost and dying world even if people don't listen?

Is it our responsibility for them to hear, to listen? Or is it our responsibility to tell the truth about Jesus? And if we hear the call, how long will we be faithful? Will we grow weary?

WHAT WILL IT TAKE TO GET OUR ATTENTION?

Isaiah heard God calling him, and he answered. But do we always hear God? Do we always listen, or does the noise of the world drown out His voice? What will it take to get our attention so we can hear God calling us to righteousness and holiness? Will we learn from Israel's example?

DAY ONE

Greetings, steadfast one. Thank you for wanting to know your God. As you begin this week in prayer, know that we're praying for you. God is raising up an army of valiant men and women of all ages who will move to the front lines, equipped for these final days. We're so thankful you're among them. You're highly esteemed in our eyes.

Read Isaiah 9:8–10:4 today, marking *Ephraim* (remember that Samaria is the capital of the northern kingdom, which is referred to here as Ephraim), *wickedness,* and *woe.*

You can't miss God in action in these verses. Be sure you mark references to God and note what you learn.

How does this passage break into sections? You can find the key repeated phrase that ends each subsection of this passage. Watch for it! You'll see it. Underline or highlight it in some way.

This phrase should help you determine a theme for Isaiah 9, which you can then record on ISAIAH AT A GLANCE on page 121.

DAY TWO

Today we're going to go deeper into Isaiah 10. This is an important text, so observe it carefully. Careful, repeated observation is the key to accurate interpretation and valid application.

Read Isaiah 10:5-34, marking *Assyria, woe,*[6] *remnant*[7] and *destroy*[8] (*destruction*). Also mark geographical and time references.

Did you get the picture? Is there anything to apply—anything you learned about God, His power, and His response to those who go beyond His purpose, who act arrogantly, and who think more than they ought to think of themselves? Think about what you learned about what God will do to Assyria. What do you learn about God?

Determine a theme for Isaiah 10 and then record it on ISAIAH AT A GLANCE.

DAY THREE

After you pray, read Isaiah 11 and mark *shoot,*[9] *branch, root* (singular) and their pronouns, all in the same way. Also mark *remnant* and time and geographical references.

List what you learn about the shoot or branch in Isaiah 11:1-5 and then summarize what conditions will be like according to Isaiah 11:6-9.

In Isaiah 11:10, what do you learn about the root of Jesse?

What do you learn about the remnant in Isaiah 11:11-16?

Finally, determine a theme for Isaiah 11 and then record it on ISAIAH AT A GLANCE.

DAY FOUR

Review your list from yesterday about the branch. Now, let's have some prophetic fun today! Look at Revelation 19:11-16 to see what else you can learn. Compare this to your list from Isaiah 11.

Also look at these cross references to learn about the remnant mentioned in Isaiah 11:

> Matthew 24:30-31
>
> Zephaniah 3:8-13
>
> Zechariah 10:6-12

List your conclusions in your notebook.

Now look at the six verses of Isaiah 12 and think about how they connect with Isaiah 11. Read Isaiah 12 and mark the time phrase *on that day*.[10]

Now determine a theme for Isaiah 12 and record it on ISAIAH AT A GLANCE.

DAY FIVE

Isaiah 13 begins a new segment we can call *Yeshayahu*

("Jehovah saves" or "Jehovah's salvation")—a segment that takes us beyond Israel to the whole earth, to the destiny of the nations.

O Beloved, do you realize that the chapters ahead tell us what will surely come to pass? What strength, what courage that will bring us from the uncertainty and fears others will face!

Let's look at God's oracles to the nations. As you begin in prayer, ask God to broaden your understanding of what's happening among the nations at this time and how you can use this knowledge of the Word to be an effective ambassador for Christ.

Read Isaiah 13 and mark every reference to *Babylon*. What is chapter 13 about?

Read Isaiah 13 again and underline *the world* and *the earth*. What will God do to them? Why?

List the descriptions of what the world, the earth, and Babylon will look like when God is finished with them. Is this shocking? What is your reaction? What do you learn about God from this?

Look for and mark time references. When will all this take place? How long will the Babylonian destruction last?

The Medo-Persian Empire (the Medes and the Persians, who lived in what is today Iran) captured Babylon (in modern Iraq) in 539 BC but did not destroy it. That event can't be what verse 17 is referring to, based on what verse 20 says. Based on the time references in the rest of the chapter, the destruction referred to in verses 17-22 must be in what day?

Determine a theme for Isaiah 13 and then record it on ISAIAH AT A GLANCE.

DAY SIX

Read Isaiah 14:1-27 and 15:1. Did you notice any references to Babylon? Do you think Isaiah 14:1-27 is part of the oracle about Babylon, or is it a separate message. Why?

Now read Isaiah 14:1-27 again and mark *the whole earth*[11] and *the nations* as before. Mark *Sheol*[12] and references to *the LORD of Hosts*.[13]

Who does the *you* in verse 3 refer to? When will this happen?

Many commentators ascribe Isaiah 14:12-16 to Satan. The King James and New King James versions translate the Hebrew *hillel* in verse 12 as "Lucifer," but other translations use "star of the morning," "morning star," or "Day Star." Verse 16 asks, "Is this the man who made the earth tremble?" From all that is said in Isaiah 13–14, what do you think? It's okay to agree or disagree. This is just food for thought and discussion!

Oh, how we wish we had time to really dig into this one and also do a detailed study of Babylon in Scripture—another controversial subject! Does *Babylon* refer to the actual nation, or is it a symbol for something else? But this is only a survey study of Isaiah, and we won't be able to look at the 300-plus references to Babylon. But if you're ever curious, here's a list you can research when you do have time:

Genesis 10:10; 11:9

Revelation 14:6-13

Revelation 16:17-21

Revelation 17

Revelation 18

Revelation 19:1-6

See what we mean? Lots of reading and lots of other study. Maybe *Behold, Jesus Is Coming* (the New Inductive Study on Revelation) would help!

Determine a theme for Isaiah 14 and then record it on ISAIAH AT A GLANCE.

<hr>

DAY SEVEN

 Store in your heart: Isaiah 11:10
Read and discuss: Isaiah 11:1-16; 14:3-27

QUESTIONS FOR DISCUSSION OR INDIVIDUAL STUDY

- Discuss what you observed about the shoot, branch, and root in Isaiah 11.

- How do you think this relates to Isaiah 9:1-7?

- What did you learn about the remnant in Isaiah 11:11-16?

- How do the remnant and shoot relate?

- Why are Babylon and the king of Babylon judged?

- What do you learn about God from His judgment of Babylon?

- What does the promise of a remnant teach you about God?

THOUGHT FOR THE WEEK

There was once a farmer who was complaining to a friend about the trouble he was having in getting his stubborn mule to move. After listening to the farmer's complaint, the friend said he knew just what to do. "Get a two-by-four and whack the mule across the head with all your might," he advised. The farmer was taken aback. "But how will that get him to move?" asked the farmer. "Well," the friend answered, "first you've got to get his attention!"

That's just a joke, but it contains a kernel of truth. Sometimes God needs to get our attention before we really listen to Him. Isaiah was listening, but do we all listen all the time? Or are we distracted by the cares of the world?

According to Isaiah 9:9, Ephraim (the northern kingdom) and Samaria (its capital) were "asserting in pride and in arrogance of heart." They thought they could rebuild their cities and replant their forests. They did not get the message God was sending them. So God raised against them adversaries from Rezin, king of Aram, and spurred them on. There were Arameans on the east and Philistines on the west.

But look at Israel's reaction. In spite of all this, they did not return to God, nor did they seek Him. So His anger did not turn away, and His hand was still stretched out. God was not finished because He knew they had not gotten the message.

So what was God's next step in getting their attention? He has already brought adversaries, the Arameans and the Philistines. Now he strikes the elders and prophets, and not only them but also the young men, the orphans and the widows. Orphans and widows? Why them? Because they are godless and evildoers. "Wait a minute!" you say. "The orphans? Children? Aren't children innocent?"

Well, not according to Scripture. All have sinned and fall short of the glory of God according to Romans 3:23. And this is because of Adam. In Adam all have sinned, even if they have not sinned in the likeness of Adam. And death spread to all men. This is called *original sin*. All mankind is born in sin and deserves death. As Romans 6:23 teaches us, the wages of sin is death.

Many people have a warped sense of justice. They don't understand biblical justice because they don't understand God's holiness and the gravity of sin. The wages of sin is death, so all deserve to die. But in the mercy of God, Jesus takes that wage, that penalty of death. Only those who believe in this gospel will live, and that life will be eternal.

Do you remember Isaiah 7:9, the message to Ahaz, king of Judah? "If you will not believe, you surely shall not last." Like the mule, Ephraim still didn't get the message, so God continued with the two-by-four treatment by creating a drought. The land burned up.

But then God will judge the nation whom He uses to judge Israel—Assyria.

Why? Because they have their own plans and motivations. You see, Assyria didn't acknowledge God or recognize that He gave them success against Samaria. They thought they could do the same to Jerusalem, and they did not understand God's protection. So God announced His judgment against Assyria.

Then in this message God gave Isaiah, the scene shifts, the time shifts, and the subject shifts ahead to a day when a remnant will live in peace.

Based on this promise of a remnant, God told Judah and Jerusalem to trust Him, just as He had counseled His people during the reigns of Abijah, Asa, and Jehoshaphat. They were to let God judge Israel's enemies—in this case, Assyria.

And God tells them why they should have hope, why they should trust God. The hope, the future of Israel, is the remnant. The idea of a remnant is introduced in Genesis with the story of Joseph in Egypt, and it reveals God's purpose for sending him there as a captive. As Joseph declared then, God sent him there before his brothers to deliver them from the famine that spread over the earth and to preserve a remnant in the earth.

God sent this same message to Israel by the prophet Amos before Isaiah began ministering in Judah. Amos declared that God would be gracious if they hated evil, loved good, and established justice. He would preserve a remnant.

And Isaiah's contemporary prophet, Micah, also brought this message. He preached that one day God will gather a remnant, their king will go before them, and the Lord will be at their head. The nations will go to Israel to learn of the Lord so they can walk in His ways.

After the Babylonian captivity, Ezra and Nehemiah led a remnant back to Jerusalem, but this is only a picture of the final remnant of the righteous. The remnant that returned after Babylon is only a physical remnant. Isaiah and later prophets speak of a later day, a time of final rest and peace for Israel, as we read in Zephaniah and Zechariah, a time when they truly know God.

Can we learn from these examples? Will we trust in ourselves, or will we rely on God?

Philistia, Moab, and Damascus

What should God do with a nation that conspires to destroy His people, to wipe out the memory of Judah?

DAY ONE

The oracles continue from one country to another. The Lord of Hosts speaks what He wants His people to know. May we hear, understand, and live in the light of truth regardless of what the nations say, think, or threaten—even if our own nation has turned its back to God.

We'll begin with the oracle to Philistia. Read Isaiah 14:28-32 and mark all time references and the key word *wail*.[14] Add *wail* to your bookmark. Its synonyms occur frequently: *crying, tears,* and *weeping.* Mark them the same way as *wail*—perhaps with a blue tear.

Read the following and list in your notebook what you learn about the Philistines:

Isaiah 2:6

Isaiah 9:12

Isaiah 11:14

The Philistines came from the sea, settling in the coastal

areas of what is modern Israel, Lebanon, and the Gaza Strip. They were enemies of Samson, Samuel, Saul, and David. Goliath was a Philistine from Gath, one of the five main Philistine cities: Ashkelon, Ashdod, Ekron, Gaza, and Gath. The Philistines worshipped Ashtoreth, Baal-zebub, and Dagon.

Review the main points of God's word to Philistia. Whatever you understood of the oracle to Philistia, see how it ends! What word is there for you and me? Where do we run when *we* are afflicted? Who or what is our bottom line? What promise holds? What never changes?

DAYS TWO & THREE

Ready for another oracle? This time it's Moab. Seek God's wisdom and understanding, and then we'll begin.

Read Isaiah 15–16 and mark the following:

- ◦ *pray* (add this to your bookmark) with a purple bowl shaded pink, like this:
- ◦ *weeping, wailing,* and *crying* with a blue tear
- ◦ *destruction*[15] (you pick this marking)
- ◦ *therefore*[16] with three red dots in a triangle like this:

- ◦ *pride* (and synonyms) with an arrow going up like this
- ◦ Also mark time references and geographical locations. Do not mark *remnant* in 15:9; 16:14 (it doesn't refer to a remnant of Israel).

Did you notice *I* and *my*? Who is the subject? What do you learn about the subject?

DAY FOUR

Who is Moab? What do you know about the people? Let's look at Moab more closely. You can read a Bible dictionary or look up the following verses:

> Genesis 19:30-38
>
> Ruth 1:1-7; 4:9-10
>
> Matthew 1:1-6

Now, what are the main points of the oracle concerning Moab? What or who is the centerpiece of this oracle? List what you learn from Isaiah 16:5.

Now determine themes for Isaiah 15 and 16 and record them on ISAIAH AT A GLANCE.

Finally, Beloved, what is God's lesson for us? What can we apply to our lives?

DAYS FIVE & SIX

Are you amazed and perhaps troubled by the uproar among the nations of the world? If so, our study of the next two chapters will be relevant for you today. You've heard of Damascus in the Bible *and* in the news, haven't you? Today you'll observe "the oracle concerning Damascus." It will be interesting and relevant because ancient Aram is present-day Syria, and the Damascus in the Bible is the Damascus in Syria you read about in the news today.

Read Isaiah 17 and 18 and mark the key words on your bookmark. If you have any time left, read the following verses to gain more insight on Damascus, recording your insights in your notebook:

2 Samuel 8:5-6

1 Kings 15:18-19

2 Kings 14:28

2 Kings 16:9

Amos 1:3-5

Isaiah 8:1-4

Now, O man, inhabitant of the world, dweller on earth—reflect on what you have seen these past two days of study. What can you apply to your life?

Don't forget to record themes for Isaiah 17 and 18 on ISAIAH AT A GLANCE.

DAY SEVEN

 Store in your heart: Isaiah 17:7

Read and discuss: Isaiah 14:28–18:7

QUESTIONS FOR DISCUSSION OR INDIVIDUAL STUDY

- ﹏ How do the nations referred to in the oracles in these chapters relate geographically?

- ﹏ What relationships do these nations have with Israel?

- ﹏ Discuss the verses that give hope amid all this judgment and destruction.

- ﹏ Where do we run when we are afflicted? What promises can we hold on to? What never changes?

ᴖ What can you apply to your life from these oracles? What have you seen that you need to pay attention to and remember in the midst of the politics of the world?

THOUGHT FOR THE WEEK

For behold, Your enemies make an uproar,
And those who hate You have exalted themselves.

They make shrewd plans against Your people,
And conspire together against Your treasured ones.

They have said, "Come, and let us wipe them out as
a nation,
That the name of Israel be remembered no more."

For they have conspired together with one mind;
Against You they make a covenant (Psalm 83:2-8).

Is this an ancient psalm only for an ancient people, or is it also for modern times? Does the prayer in these verses strike a chord with events today, or should we relegate it to the dustbin of ancient poetry, to a time long past and forgotten? Does it relate to our study of Isaiah 14:28–18:7? What have Philistia, Moab, and Damascus done to Israel to deserve judgment? And how does that relate to today?

PHILISTIA

Philistia is the land of the Philistines, who, according to Genesis 10:14, were descended from Noah's son Ham. Historians believe they were from the island of Crete and settled on the coastland of Canaan, what is today Israel. Their territory was on the boundary of the land allocated to the tribe of Dan as an inheritance. The most famous judge from Dan was Samson, who had many encounters with the Philistines: killing 30 men in Ashkelon, tearing out the gates of the city of Gaza, encountering Delilah, and destroying the temple of Dagon in Gaza. The Philistines continued to oppress Israel from the days of the judges to the days of Saul and David.

More than 1000 years after David's reign, around AD 130, the Jews attempted to throw off Roman rule. The Roman emperor Hadrian defeated the uprising and vowed to eliminate the memory of the Jews by destroying Jerusalem, rebuilding it as a Roman city called "Aelia Capitolina," and renaming the Roman province of Judea "Syria Palestina," or Syria of the Philistines. From that time forward, the most common name for the land of Israel was "Palestine," and the people were called "Palestinians." Those people are not descendants of the Philistines. They migrated to that land much later, but the memory of the Philistines pervades vocabulary even to this day.

MOAB

After God destroyed Sodom and Gomorrah because of their gross immorality, Lot's two daughters had sons by him to perpetuate the family. These sons were named Moab and Ammon, so the Moabites were related to the Israelites.

When the Israelites came out of captivity in Egypt in the days of Moses, they asked the Moabites for passage through their lands. But Moab took action against Israel, hiring the prophet Balaam to curse Israel. They enticed Israel with their idolatry and sexual immorality in worship. Moab continued as an enemy of Israel through the days of David and to the divided kingdom.

Today, the traditional lands of Moab are part of modern-day Jordan, east of the Dead Sea. Jordan fought against Israel in the 1948 War of Independence and in the Six-Day War of

1967. From 1948 to 1967, Jordan occupied the Old City of Jerusalem, and like Hadrian nearly 2000 years earlier, Jordan kept the Jews from living in the Old City, destroying synagogues, houses, and other signs of Jewish presence in the city. The city was separated from the Jews by a barbed wire barrier, with snipers stationed on the walls of the Old City to shoot at Jews in West Jerusalem.

DAMASCUS

Damascus was the capital city of the ancient kingdom of Aram in the time of Isaiah. Aram was a pagan nation, worshipping man-made gods. David warred against Aram, and Rezin, king of Aram, was an enemy of Solomon. Aram continued as an enemy of Israel and Judah throughout the days of the divided kingdom.

Although God used Aram at various times to try to get Israel and Judah to trust Him, ultimately He judged the nation. Amos prophesied, "For three transgressions of Damascus and for four I will not revoke its punishment, because they threshed Gilead with implements of sharp iron" (Amos 1:3).

Today, Damascus is the capital of Syria, which fought Israel in the 1948 War of Independence, the 1967 Six-Day War, and the 1973 Yom Kippur War. Syria sponsors the terrorist organization Hezbollah, which has sworn to destroy Israel.

So the judgments in Isaiah against these nations for their opposition to Israel perhaps extend even to today. And if these nations continue in their opposition to Israel, as the Scripture seems to indicate they will, they will face judgment from God in that day when He comes to judge the nations.

The question of application for us is this: Are we like these nations? Are we in opposition to God's chosen people?

Not everything the modern political nation of Israel does is right, just as ancient Israel didn't always follow God. But these nations will be judged for oppressing Israel, for conspiring to wipe them out as a nation, so what about us? What about the nation you live in? This food for thought gives us reason to know the plans of God.

WHO IS BEHIND STRIKING AND HEALING?

Have you ever been struck…then healed? Who was behind it? What lesson is there in this? Who is in control of life and the affairs of mankind? And what does God want from us?

DAY ONE

When you think of Egypt, what comes to mind? Is it Israel's 400-year slavery, Pharaoh's hardened heart, and his refusal to let God's people go? Or do you think of Israel's present-day enemy to the south? What is Egypt's future? You may be surprised. Let's see what God tells us through Isaiah the prophet as we continue our study of the oracles concerning the nations.

After prayer, read Isaiah 19–20. Then read Isaiah 19 again and mark the key words on your bookmark. Also mark these:

> *purpose*[17] (*purposed*[18]) (Don't add these two to your bookmark.)

sign

Assyria

Egypt

That's enough for today; give your brain and hands a rest!

DAY TWO

Begin your study today by listing what you learned about God from Isaiah 19.

What will happen in Egypt "in that day"? What is God's purpose for Egypt? What will happen to Egypt, Assyria, and Israel?

Record a theme for Isaiah 19 on ISAIAH AT A GLANCE.

Now read Isaiah 20 and mark key words. How is this chapter different from the oracles before it?

Determine a theme for Isaiah 20 and record it on ISAIAH AT A GLANCE.

DAY THREE

Read Isaiah 21 to get an overview. Mark each reference to a new *oracle* (or *burden* in some translations) distinctly.

Read Isaiah 21 again, marking key words from your bookmark. Also mark these, but don't add them to your bookmark: *terrifying*[19] (*treacherous*[20]) and *watchman* (*watchtower*). Don't forget to mark the synonyms and pronouns.

DAY FOUR

What do you learn about Isaiah in chapter 21? Look at *I, my,* and *me.* Is it easy to be a prophet?

Assyria is front and center, the predominant power in the first 39 chapters of Isaiah. Babylon is more prominent in the last section of the book, yet here's another reference to Babylon. What do you learn from marking *Babylon?*

Edom is part of modern-day Jordan, and Arabia is modern Saudi Arabia. What is the point of the oracle concerning Edom?

What will happen to Arabia and why?

Can you apply anything in this chapter to your life?

Record a theme for chapter 21 and add it to ISAIAH AT A GLANCE.

DAY FIVE

We have two more chapters to study in these last two days, as we want to divide our homework according to the division in Isaiah. Today you'll observe the oracle concerning the valley of vision. What is this valley? Who or what is this oracle about? Read Isaiah 22 and see what the text tells you.

Now observe Isaiah 22. Mark the key words on your bookmark as well as *planned*[21] (mark it as you marked *purposed* in chapter 19). Mark *therefore* (other translations use other words in verse 12) and note the train of thought. Mark *weeping* (*wailing*[22]) and observe who is weeping and why. Mark *depended*[23] (*depend*) and note who is depending on whom in each usage.

What verse best summarizes the problem with the people of Judah? Do you see this today among Christians? Do you see it in yourself?

Finally, record a theme for Isaiah 22 on ISAIAH AT A GLANCE.

This chapter has much to teach us about Tyre and its significance in biblical times. Observe Isaiah 23, marking key words from your bookmark. Also mark the commands in verses 1-2,4,6, and 14—including the repeated one to the ships of Tarshish. (This is where Jonah was fleeing when he rebelled against going to Nineveh in Assyria. It's probably modern-day Spain.)

Also mark *pride* (especially verse 9), its synonym *exult*[24] (in verse 12), and *planned*.[25]

Finally, determine a theme for Isaiah 23 and record it on ISAIAH AT A GLANCE.

 Store in your heart: Isaiah 19:20

Read and discuss: Isaiah 19:16-25; 21:1-10; 22:1-14; 23:8-15

QUESTIONS FOR DISCUSSION OR INDIVIDUAL STUDY

- ∾ Discuss your insights about God's purposes for Egypt.

- ∾ How hard is it to be a prophet? What insights did you gain from Isaiah's words? What is the prophet's role? Compare this to Isaiah 6:8-13.

- ∾ What will God do with Israel? Will He treat them the same way as He treated Egypt, Edom, Moab, Aram, Arabia, and Philistia, or will He treat Israel differently? Why?

 ∾ What general principles can you draw from these chapters about God and His purposes for man?

 ∾ What applications can you make in your own life from these principles? Are they true today and for the future, or just for the time of Isaiah? Why?

THOUGHT FOR THE WEEK

Last week, we studied the oracles concerning Philistia, Moab, and Damascus in Isaiah 14:28–18:7. Isaiah announced God's judgment against these nations because they failed to worship God. God had intended for these nations to bring about Israel's return to Him, and they should have recognized His hand at work and given credit to Him. They also should have recognized that Israel was God's chosen people, and they should not have reached out their hand to strike God's anointed.

This week, we studied the oracles concerning Egypt, Babylon, Edom, Arabia, and Tyre in Isaiah 19–23. We see the same points we saw last week, but these chapters contain another message as well: No one can thwart God's plan. What He has purposed will come to pass. Why? Because He is God.

And why does God warn us so? Look at what the prophet Amos said:

> Hear this word which the LORD has spoken
> against you, sons of Israel, against the entire family
> which He brought up from the land of Egypt:
>
> "You only have I chosen among all the
>   families of the earth;
> Therefore I will punish you for all your
>   iniquities."

Do two men walk together unless they have
    made an appointment?

Does a lion roar in the forest when he has no
    prey?

Does a young lion growl from his den unless
    he has captured something?

Does a bird fall into a trap on the ground when
    there is no bait in it?

Does a trap spring up from the earth when it
    captures nothing at all?

If a trumpet is blown in a city, will not the
    people tremble?

If a calamity occurs in a city has not the Lord
    done it?

Surely the Lord God does nothing
Unless He reveals His secret counsel
To His servants the prophets.

A lion has roared! Who will not fear?
The Lord God has spoken! Who can but
    prophesy? (Amos 3:1-8).

In Isaiah 19, in the oracle concerning Egypt, God demonstrates control over nature and man. In verses 5-10, we can see that we are not to trust in nature, but in God. Nature was created by God, and it was good, but the earth was cursed as a consequence of Adam's fall (Genesis 3). Now the earth groans for its redemption (Romans 8:19-22).

In verses 11-14, we can see we are to trust not in man's wisdom but in God's. In the first two chapters of 1 Corinthians, Paul shows that Christ Himself is our wisdom, the wisdom of God. This wisdom appears foolish compared to man's worldly wisdom, but it actually shows man's foolishness and lack of power. Paul writes in 1 Corinthians 2:4-5 that our faith is not to rest on man's wisdom:

> And my message and my preaching were not in persuasive words of wisdom, but in demonstration of the Spirit and of power, so that your faith would not rest on the wisdom of men, but on the power of God.

The phrase "in that day" in Isaiah 19:16 signals a change. The Lord of hosts moves in Egypt and Assyria to save those peoples. The purpose of the Lord will be made clear to all nations.

How much this is like the period of the judges. When Israel walked in wickedness, God sent an oppressor to cause them to turn to Him. Then when they cried out to Him, He sent a deliverer, a judge. See how much God wants people to trust Him, to rely upon Him, to worship Him? Not only Israel but also Egypt and Assyria are to turn to God in faith and trust and dependence. God uses whatever means necessary to show people they cannot trust in nature or in man's wisdom, but must turn to Him. He will strike, but He will heal. And they will worship Him.

That's what God wants from all mankind—for people everywhere to turn to Him in worship.

The key idea is God's purpose. What was God's purpose in Joseph being taken to Egypt? Joseph himself answered that question in Genesis 50:20: "As for you, you meant evil against me, but God meant it for good in order to bring about this present result, to preserve many people alive."

Why did God afflict Job? Job 1–2 clearly shows that His purpose was to demonstrate to Satan that his view of man—that man was faithful to God only because God blessed him—was wrong, a lie born out of Satan's own nature. Job showed Satan that man could worship God even when severely afflicted from loss of possessions, family, and health. Job trusted God—not nature and not man's wisdom.

Why did God allow Assyria to defeat the northern kingdom? To show Judah what will happen to those who worship idols rather than God. He was warning them that He *would* take them into captivity to discipline them. He wanted them to turn back from their idolatry and their arrogant self-confidence that they would stay in Jerusalem and Judah and not to be taken captive.

What does God ultimately want? He wants us to swear allegiance to Him and to keep our word. He wants obedience. Look at what Samuel says about obedience:

> Has the LORD as much delight in burnt
>   offerings and sacrifices
> As in obeying the voice of the LORD?
> Behold, to obey is better than sacrifice,
> And to heed than the fat of rams.
>
> For rebellion is as the sin of divination,
> And insubordination is as iniquity and
>   idolatry (1 Samuel 15:22-23).

God wants us to understand His purposes, to worship and obey Him no matter what. He strikes and heals to show that we can trust no one and nothing besides Him.

WILL THE UNGODLY TRIUMPH IN THE END?

Do you get weary and discouraged when the ungodly seem to triumph? When nations deny Christ and do not allow their people to freely worship Him without reprisal? Do you wonder when or if these things will ever come to an end? What will bring true peace?

DAY ONE

O Beloved, what a special week of study awaits you! Meditate; savor the truths in your heart. Remember, these are the very words of God. God is speaking, not man. Hear the Word of the Lord and fill your time with worship.

Read Isaiah 24 today, marking *Lord* and the key words on your bookmark. Also mark *earth*, including pronouns. Color it brown and double underline in green as you do all geographical locations. Mark *covenant* and add it to your bookmark. *Curse* is used only once, but it's significant. Also mark *glory* (*glorify*).

DAY TWO

List everything you learned about the earth in Isaiah 24. Then read the following, marking *earth* and *covenant:*

Genesis 6:11-18

Genesis 9:8-17

2 Peter 3:3-15

Look at the time phrases you marked in Isaiah 24. What do you see?

What contrast did you see in Isaiah 24:16? Why the woes?

Finally, determine a theme for Isaiah 24 and record it on ISAIAH AT A GLANCE.

If you have the time, read Revelation 6:1-17; 8:1–9:21; 11:15-19; 12:7-12; 16:1-21; 19:11-21; Zechariah 14:1-9. Can you determine how any of these relate to Isaiah?

DAY THREE

After beginning in prayer, read Isaiah 25, marking the words on your bookmark. Add *mountain* (remember, *mountain of the Lord, Jerusalem,* and *Zion* are synonymous). Also mark *death* (You could use a black tombstone like this ⌂ .

Now list your insights about the Lord and what He is going to do according to Isaiah 24–25. By the way, did you notice what the Lord made a city into, what the "cities of ruthless nations" will do, and why? This might help you interpret *city* in Isaiah 24.

Now read Isaiah 25 again and bask in the Lord's holiness and goodness.

Remember when you marked *planned* and *purposed* last week? Now compare what 25:1 says about the Lord with what you learned last week. Also compare Ephesians 1:4-11.

What are people saved from (25:9)?

Remember to record a theme for chapter 25 on ISAIAH AT A GLANCE.

DAY FOUR

Remember, Isaiah 24–27 is a unit. Read it together so you don't lose sight of what God is doing. Note what connects chapter 25 with chapter 26.

Now read Isaiah 26, another wonderful chapter to observe, and one that begins with a song. As you read, mark these:

> *peace* (Add this to your key word bookmark.)
>
> *trust*
>
> *righteous(ness)*[26] (Add this to your bookmark.)
>
> *the earth*
>
> *dead* (Note what you observe.)

What spoke to you the most as you observed this chapter? What is your prayer?

Record a theme for Isaiah 26 on ISAIAH AT A GLANCE.

DAY FIVE

Contrast the wicked and the righteous in Isaiah 26—their hearts and their behavior.

What did you learn about the dead in verse 14? What does verse 19 tell us about the dead? What happens to them? Does this affect all the dead? Do you see any differences between verses 14 and 19?

Read the following to see what you learn about the dead:

Daniel 12:2

Job 19:25-27

John 5:24-29

Revelation 20:4-6,11-15

Revelation 21:1-8

Now, remembering what you learned in Isaiah 25:8, what is the future of the dead?

DAY SIX

Well, we've come to the final chapter of this unique segment in Isaiah. How does it connect to Isaiah 26? Read Isaiah 27, marking the key words from your bookmark. Also mark *Jacob* (*Israel*).

Again, list what you learned about the Lord. When you finish, take a few minutes to thank God for revealing these truths to you.

Look at how this segment (Isaiah 24–27) begins and ends. What does it follow? How does Isaiah 24 open? What is the focus? What is the focus of Isaiah 27?

According to what you've seen, what is Israel's condition on the day the Lord comes from His place to punish the inhabitants of the earth for their iniquity? How is Israel able to gain favor with God?

Look at the time references to *that day* in Isaiah 26:20–27:13. What do you learn?

Record a theme for Isaiah 27 on ISAIAH AT A GLANCE.

DAY SEVEN

Store in your heart: Isaiah 26:3

Read and discuss: Isaiah 24:1-6,21-23; 25:6-9; 26:1-10,19-21; 27:12-13

QUESTIONS FOR DISCUSSION OR INDIVIDUAL STUDY

- ∞ Discuss the judgment on the earth.

- ∞ What did you learn about death? What will God do?

- ∞ What is the significance of the phrase *in that day?* What happens then?

- ∞ How does God give hope to Israel, to the nations, and to you in these chapters?

- ∞ Talk about the righteous, the unrighteous, and God's judgment. Can you relate this to today?

- ∞ In the midst of judgment for iniquity, can you find peace? How do you achieve peace? What do you know about the Lord from this lesson that will help you?

THOUGHT FOR THE WEEK

Nearly 4000 years ago in Egypt, the patriarch Jacob gathered his 12 sons and said, "Assemble yourselves that I may tell you what will befall you in the days to come" (Genesis 49:1).

One by one he described the future for his sons, but in verse 18 he added, "For Your salvation I wait, O LORD." As Jacob was blessing his sons and prophesying, God put the idea of salvation in Jacob's heart. This is the first time *salvation* is used in the Bible. It occurs 160 times in all.

Already in Isaiah we have read this:

> "Behold, God is my salvation,
> I will trust and not be afraid;
> For the LORD GOD is my strength and song,
> And He has become my salvation."

> Therefore you will joyously draw water
> From the springs of salvation (Isaiah 12:2-3).

> For you have forgotten the God of your salvation
> And have not remembered the rock of your refuge.
> Therefore you plant delightful plants
> And set them with vine slips of a strange god
> (Isaiah 17:10).

And now we see this in this week's lesson:

> And it will be said in that day,
> "Behold, this is our God for whom we have
>   waited that He might save us.
> This is the LORD for whom we have waited;
> Let us rejoice and be glad in His salvation"
> (Isaiah 25:9).

Why does anyone need salvation? Salvation from what?

The answer lies in Genesis 3. In the garden of Eden, the serpent, Satan, tempted Adam and Eve to doubt and to disregard God's word. They disobeyed God and sinned. In that day, they died spiritually, although they would live physically for many more years. They realized then that they were naked and were ashamed, and they hid from God. Romans 5 tells us that the sin of Adam spread to all mankind, even to those who did not sin as Adam did. Death spread to all mankind because of Adam's sin.

In Genesis 3, God cursed the serpent, Adam and Eve, and the earth. From that day on, mankind and creation has groaned for redemption from this curse of death.

How long did the world have to wait?

In the days of Noah, God saw the evil intent of men's hearts and the sin that they lived in, and He was sorry that He made man. He judged the earth with a flood that killed all living creatures except those who took refuge in the ark.

After the flood, God made a covenant with all living creatures, with man, and with the earth: He promised not to destroy the earth with water again.

How does this relate to Isaiah? Consider what we have seen in this lesson. Isaiah 24:5 tells us that "the earth is also polluted by its inhabitants, for they transgressed laws, violated statutes, broke the everlasting covenant."

But we know from Genesis 9 that God will not destroy the earth with water again. What will He use? How will God judge the earth? Second Peter 3:3-15 shows us that the present heavens and earth will burn up. Fire will dissolve the corrupt earth. Eight times the Bible tells us that God is a consuming fire.

When we think about fire, we should remember that fire is used to purify. In Leviticus, fire was used to purify gold, silver, and precious stones. But fire burns up other things, so water was used to cleanse those.

This is interesting to think about because the New Testament talks about our works being tested to see if they endure or burn up like wood, hay, or stubble. Our treasure is to be in heaven, an imperishable treasure, not like things on earth that rust or are eaten by moths (Matthew 6:19-20).

And if we think about the change in our bodies described in 1 Corinthians 15, the perishable must put on the imperishable, the mortal must put on the immortal. The new heaven and earth will be imperishable. That which is perishable (or mortal) will die, which is why we see the quotation of Isaiah 25:8 in 1 Corinthians 15:54.

How long will Israel have to wait for salvation? They waited from the days of Isaiah until the first coming of Jesus, but they didn't recognize Him or receive Him according to John 1:11. But when He returns, they will see Him, as Zechariah 12:10 says.

And when He comes again, He will judge the living and the dead, righteousness will reign, and those who sow iniquity will reap their reward. In the end, the wicked will not triumph. And peace will reign.

When You're Confronted with a Problem, Where Do You Turn?

∾∾∾∾

When you're confronted with a problem, when you need to make a decision, when an adversary rises up against you, what's your first response? Where do you turn? Do you do what you should do? And what's that?

DAY ONE

Isaiah 28 tells of the glorious beauty of Ephraim at the head of the fertile valley. Isaiah 28 is rich, and you'll want to read it and Isaiah 29 again and again so that their message lodges not only in your mind but also in your heart. Remember, we learn from Israel's example. Spend today observing Isaiah 28, marking the words on your bookmark.

In addition, mark *knowledge*.[27] You can color it a deep green. Mark *the word of the Lord* and any other references to God speaking. This is especially significant to the message of this chapter. Mark *stone (cornerstone),* but you don't need to put this on your bookmark. Finally, mark *listen*[28] *(hear)* and put it on your bookmark.

Look at what you marked with respect to God speaking and the people listening. In a sentence or two, record what you observed. Then examine your life and your walk with God.

Record a theme for Isaiah 28 on ISAIAH AT A GLANCE.

DAY TWO

What did you learn yesterday about the stone? Read the following and add to your insights:

Isaiah 8:13-15

Romans 9:33

Psalm 118:22

1 Peter 2:6-8

Acts 4:8-12

Daniel 2:31-45

Also read Matthew 21:33-46 and note the context of the stone. Answer all the 5 W's and H questions you can from this passage. (You can find parallel passages in Mark and Luke.)

What parallels do you see between Daniel's and Isaiah's references to the stone?

Let's also look at *destruction,* which you should have marked because it was on your bookmark. Review what you saw in Isaiah 10:20-25 and compare it to what you saw in Isaiah 28. What do you remember about destruction in Revelation?

How does Revelation 3:10 compare to Isaiah 28:22?

Lastly, take a look at Daniel 7:19-27 and note what is going to happen to the whole earth and then whose kingdom is coming.

DAY THREE

Read Isaiah 29 and underline in pencil the references to *Ariel,* including pronouns. Can you tell who or what Ariel is? List what you learn about Ariel.

Now read Isaiah 29 again, marking key words from your bookmark.

What war is mentioned? Who will participate in it? Compare this war to the one in Isaiah 7. Is it the same?

Read Joel 3:9-21; Zechariah 14:1-9; Matthew 24:15-31; and Revelation 16:12-16. What do these have in common?

Finally, determine a theme for Isaiah 29 and record it on ISAIAH AT A GLANCE.

DAY FOUR

After you seek the Lord in prayer for His wisdom and understanding, read Isaiah 30:1; 31:1; and 33:1. What do you discern? What key word needs to be marked?

Now read Isaiah 30 and mark key words as usual. *Egypt(ians)* is a key word, so mark it as you have before. Remember that we began Isaiah 19 with God's oracle regarding Egypt. You'll also want to mark *Pharaoh* the same way because he represents Egypt. Don't forget to mark references to *hearing* and *listening.* Think about what you have learned. Is there any application here? If so, what?

Is the focus of the chapter Egypt, or is it Israel? What shift or change in the message do you see, and where? How does the chapter begin, and how does it end? What is the future of Israel, the nations, and Assyria?

Record a theme for Isaiah 30 on ISAIAH AT A GLANCE.

DAYS FIVE & SIX

Read Isaiah 31, marking key words, including *Egypt, war,*[29] and *return.*

Analyze what's happening in this chapter. List themes for each of these sections:

> Isaiah 31:1-3
>
> Isaiah 31:4-5
>
> Isaiah 31:6-9

Record a theme for Isaiah 31 on ISAIAH AT A GLANCE.

What do you think "whose fire is in Zion and whose furnace is in Jerusalem" means?

Isaiah 32 doesn't start with "woe," but how is it connected to Isaiah 30–31? Read the chapter and mark *fool,*[30] *rogue,*[31] *noble,*[32] and *women.* Mark the time phrases (watch for *until* and *then*).

Mark reference to *the Spirit* of the Lord. It is good to mark every reference in your Bible to the Spirit because there's so much misunderstanding. Recording what you learn will help you develop a biblical theology of the Spirit.

Finally, mark *righteousness* and record a theme for Isaiah 32 on ISAIAH AT A GLANCE.

DAY SEVEN

 Store in your heart: Isaiah 31:1

Read and discuss: Isaiah 30–32

QUESTIONS FOR DISCUSSION OR INDIVIDUAL STUDY

∾ Discuss what you learned about trusting in Egypt versus trusting in God.

∾ What is the contrast between those who trust in the Lord and those who don't?

∾ What did you learn about the Lord this week?

∾ What is the clearest word the Lord gave you for your life this week? Is there anything you need to do, remember, or change?

∾ What change occurs in the culture in Isaiah 32:3-8? What values change? What happens to the people? How does this relate to the New Testament? To today, to you and me?

∾ Discuss the call to action in Isaiah 32:9-20. How does it relate to today?

THOUGHT FOR THE WEEK

Isaiah 28–32 includes a lot of talk about judgment, woe, destruction, and the like. This judgment is from the Lord, so it is a sure judgment. What He says will come to pass does come to pass. But there's also talk of hope in these chapters, and because this hope is from the Lord, it too is sure.

Unfortunately, though, some people will suffer judgment because they just won't listen; they won't see the truth that is right in front of their eyes. Israel is like that. So are Assyria and the other nations. When we read in Isaiah 28 that God promises to lay a stone in Zion, and that whoever believes in it will not be disturbed, we rejoice because there is hope for Israel. But we also grieve over their blindness. The stone laid 2000 years ago was also a stone for stumbling, rejected by the builders.

God had been teaching Israel from its earliest days that He is a rock of refuge, a rock that they could rely on. He is a rock unlike any other.

In Exodus 17 and again in Numbers 20, God miraculously provided the Israelites with water from a rock. First Corinthians 10:1-5 informs us that the rock following them was Jesus, who gives life-giving water. They were drinking from Him, but they were not satisfied with Him. He is our salvation, but to the Jews He was a stone of stumbling, a rock of offense because "they did not pursue [righteousness] by faith, but as though it were by works. They stumbled over the stumbling stone, just as it is written, Behold, I lay in Zion a stone of stumbling and a rock of offense, And he who believes in Him will not be disappointed" (Romans 9:32-33).

Jesus was the stone the builders rejected, according to 1 Peter 2:4-8. Peter quotes Isaiah 28:16 and explains that Jesus is the cornerstone of a spiritual house. But Jesus was rejected by men, as Peter shows by quoting Psalm 118:22: "The stone which the builders rejected has become the chief corner stone." Peter also quotes Isaiah 8:14 to show that this stone was "'a stone of stumbling and a rock of offense'; for they stumble because they are disobedient to the word, and to this doom they were also appointed."

That was because they chose the wrong foundation. Instead of building on solid rock, they built their houses on sand—the keeping of the law instead of believing in Christ.

Jesus told a story in His Sermon on the Mount to illustrate the principle of building on solid rock instead of sand, so that when wind and flood come, the house will stand and not be washed away. The foundation Jesus referred to was hearing and obeying His words. And we know that His words include the truth that He is God, the Son of God, the one in whom to believe for salvation.

Ephesians 2:20 instructs us that we are "built on the foundation of the apostles and prophets, Christ Jesus Himself being the corner stone." And in Acts 4, Peter preached this in a sermon in the temple: "He is the stone which was rejected by you, the builders, but which became the chief corner stone" (Acts 4:11).

That is the solid foundation on which anyone can stand, the Rock in which anyone can take refuge in time of distress or trouble, the Rock who gives hope. And although Israel rejected Jesus when He came the first time, when He comes the second time, the remnant will recognize Him. According to Zechariah 12:10, "I [God] will pour out on the house of David and on the inhabitants of Jerusalem, the Spirit of grace and of supplication, so that they will look on Me whom they have pierced; and they will mourn for Him, as one mourns for an only son, and they will weep bitterly over Him like the bitter weeping over a firstborn."

Zechariah 13:8-9 goes on to give this hope for Israel: " 'It will come about in all the land,' declares the LORD, 'That two parts in it will be cut off and perish; but the third will be left in it. And I will bring the third part through the fire, refine them as silver is refined, and test them as gold is tested. They will call on My name, and I will answer them; I will say, "They are My people," And they will say, "The LORD is my God." ' "

There is hope!

*W*HAT *H*APPENS *W*HEN *Y*OU *P*RAY?

What can you do when life feels like a marathon and you're exhausted? What can you say when a friend or family member is ready to give up the race and collapse in a heap? What happens when you pray? And what happens when you don't?

DAY ONE

Read Isaiah 33:1–36:10. From your cursory reading, note how 33:1 begins. What is the focus of Isaiah 34? What is Isaiah 35 about? What's happening in the first ten verses of Isaiah 36?

Read Isaiah 33 again, marking key words and paying attention to who is destroyed and why. Watch for references to the person and actions of the Lord. Note what the people see and don't see. You may want to mark *see* and *behold.*

What do you learn about the Lord?

DAY TWO

Read through Isaiah 34 and mark *nations.* What's said to

and about them is very important. Also mark *Edom*.[33] Much
is said, so don't miss any pronouns. Mark *Edom* in red in
some way.

Edom has been mentioned twice in Isaiah so far (11:14;
21:11-12), but we didn't stop to study Edom then. We don't
have time to do an exhaustive study about Edom, but here
are a few verses to observe:

> Genesis 25:23-34
>
> Numbers 20:14-21
>
> Obadiah 1

If you have time and want to do more study, also look at
Jeremiah 49:7-22; Ezekiel 35:1-15; and Psalm 137:7 (but read
this last verse in the context of the whole psalm. It was written
after the Babylonians destroyed Jerusalem in 586 BC).

DAY THREE

Read Isaiah 35 and mark geographical references,
including *Zion*. Locate these places on the map in the back
of this book. *Arabah* can mean a desert, as it is translated in
the KJV, NKJV, and ESV, or it can mean a wilderness, as it is
translated in the NIV.

Mark *redeemed*. This word (and *Redeemer*) will be key
from this point on in Isaiah, so put it on your bookmark. Up
to this point, *redeemed* has been used only in Isaiah 1:27 and
29:22.

List the instructions (commands) in verses 3-4.

Mark *highway*[34] *of Holiness* and note who walks on it and
who doesn't.

Compare Isaiah 35 with Isaiah 29:17-24. What do you

see? After the woes, what do Isaiah 29:17-24 and Isaiah 35 give the reader and how?

Record your themes for Isaiah 33–35 on ISAIAH AT A GLANCE.

DAY FOUR

In Isaiah 1–35, God promises His ultimate intervention and salvation. His grace follows His righteous judgments on His people Israel and the nations. But what about now? You'll find your answer to this question in the next few days, which will conclude our study of this first segment (chapters 1–39) of Isaiah.

Read Isaiah 36–39 as a unit. List the major events and characters of each chapter. How do these chapters differ from most of the chapters you studied in Isaiah 1–35? Which chapters in Isaiah 1–35 do Isaiah 36–39 remind you of? How?

Now read Isaiah 36, marking the key words on your bookmark, geographical references, and time indicators. Also mark *Rabshakeh* and observe his method of operation very carefully.

Record a theme for this chapter on ISAIAH AT A GLANCE.

Now read 2 Kings 18, a parallel passage that will give you additional insights into Isaiah 36. What additional insights into Hezekiah do you find?

DAY FIVE

Read Isaiah 37 and mark the main characters (including Assyria) and geographical and time references. Mark *the Holy*

One of Israel and note the setting it's used in. Also pay careful attention to how Hezekiah addresses God. Mark *prayer* and ask the 5 W's and an H. Finally, mark *remnant* and *sign.*

Determine a theme for this chapter on ISAIAH AT A GLANCE.

DAY SIX

Read Isaiah 38, marking time phrases, *death,* and *sin.*

Watch the relationship of verses 9-22 to verses 1-8. How would you divide this chapter and why?

Compare Isaiah 38:1-8 with 2 Kings 20:1-7 and 2 Chronicles 32:24-26. What did you learn?

Now read Isaiah 39 and mark the key words from your bookmark. Don't miss the time references.

Now read 2 Chronicles 32:27-31. What insight into Isaiah 39 does this give you?

Well, that's it for this week, Beloved! Don't forget to record themes for Isaiah 38 and 39 on ISAIAH AT A GLANCE.

DAY SEVEN

 Store in your heart: Isaiah 35:10

Read and discuss: Isaiah 33:2-24; 34:1-8; 35:1-10; 36:1-18; 37:1-7,14-20,36-38; 38:1-8; 39:1-8

QUESTIONS FOR DISCUSSION OR INDIVIDUAL STUDY

∾ Discuss the triumph of the Lord amid all the judgment and distress you've seen so far in Isaiah. Is there any application to your life?

∾ Discuss the righteous judgment of God against the nations and Edom. What will happen? Why? Is the answer in Isaiah 34, in earlier chapters of Isaiah, in other books of the Bible?

∾ What kinds of things can you use from Isaiah 35 to encourage others when they are discouraged, when life has worn them down? When will these things occur?

∾ Have you ever been in a desperate situation like Hezekiah with the Assyrians? Discuss Rabshakeh's tactics. How are they like Satan's tactics? What should you do when you are in a similar situation?

∾ Discuss Hezekiah's illness, his reaction, and God's answer through Isaiah. Have you ever been in a situation like Hezekiah? How did you respond? And what did God do?

∾ Discuss the incident between Hezekiah and the Babylonians in Isaiah 39. Was Hezekiah wrong? How do you know? What were the consequences? Did Hezekiah understand?

THOUGHT FOR THE WEEK

Isaiah begins this way: "The vision of Isaiah the son of Amoz concerning Judah and Jerusalem, which he saw during the reigns of Uzziah, Jotham, Ahaz and Hezekiah, kings of Judah."

We've looked at 39 chapters of this vision. We've seen oracles, woes, and judgments on the northern kingdom of Israel, Aram, Assyria, Babylon, Moab, Egypt, Tyre, Sidon, the nations, the earth, and even Judah and Jerusalem.

We've also seen the promises of hope for the remnant of Israel, for those who will believe God.

There are really only two points for mankind to learn in these chapters: judgment on sin and hope for those who believe God, those who trust Him and not themselves. Isaiah delivered this message from God for almost 60 years, never seeing the fulfillment of the promised hope even though he saw the beginning of the promised judgments. The time of Isaiah's vision includes the demise of the northern kingdom of Israel, ending with its captivity by Assyria in 722 BC.

With all these oracles, woes, and judgments, I wonder if anyone in the days of Isaiah thought it was really possible to please God, to trust Him and be spared from judgment? After all, the prophecies about Israel and Aram were fulfilled, at least in part, as Assyria came to defeat Aram and take Israel captive.

People can easily see that God's promised judgment came. But what about His promised hope for those who believe? Was there any reason to believe that would come to pass?

Well, let's look at our four kings to see what we can learn from their stories. King Uzziah was 16 years old when he began to reign, and he reigned 52 years ending in 739 BC, the year Isaiah's ministry began. Kings and Chronicles inform us that he did right in the sight of the Lord, but the high places were not removed, so the people still worshiped false gods. He continued to seek God in the days of Zechariah, and God helped him fight Philistines and Arabians. But when he became strong, his heart became proud, and he acted corruptly. He was unfaithful to God, even entering the temple to burn incense. For that offense against God, he was a leper the rest of his life, and his son Jotham ruled in his place.

So the people saw a good king, who was faithful to God, go astray at the end of his life because his heart became proud when he achieved success. He didn't give God credit for his success.

Jotham did right in the sight of God; he did not enter the

temple like his father had. But the people continued acting corruptly, so he did not remove high places. He built fortifications and prevailed over Ammon, and he became mighty. Nothing about those times was particularly remarkable, except that he reigned during the time that Assyria began to take parts of the northern kingdom (Israel) captive.

His son Ahaz was the next king in Judah. He was one of Judah's most wicked kings. Therefore God delivered him into the hands of Aram and Israel.

Ahaz's son Hezekiah became king during the reign of Hoshea, the last king of Israel. That means he was king from at least 728–722 BC, witnessing the captivity of Israel. This was most likely a co-regency with his father. Sennacherib came against Judah in 701 BC, in the "fourteenth year of his reign," which can only be counted from the death of Ahaz and the start of his sole reign in 715 BC.

After the reign of Ahaz, did the citizens of Jerusalem and Judah have any hope? Would son be like father, doomed to follow in his awful footsteps?

The life of Hezekiah shows us that there is hope. We are not doomed. At the beginning of the 29 years he reigned after his father died, he led a great revival, opening the doors to the temple that Ahaz had closed, cleansing the temple, and restoring the priesthood. He held a great Passover, which hadn't been celebrated in years.

When Assyria came against Judah in the fourteenth year of his reign, Hezekiah cried out to God, and God delivered Judah from Assyria. Here was evidence that a man could restore trust in his God, and God would bless him. God protected him from his enemies and from an illness. So we know it's possible to resist a proud heart, to repent, to return to faith, to remain faithful, to trust in God in difficult circumstances against an enemy and in illness.

If Hezekiah can do it, then so can you and I. Unlike

Hezekiah, we have a resident power within us, the Holy Spirit. We also have the promise of 1 John 1:9: "If we confess our sins, He is faithful and righteous to forgive us our sins and to cleanse us from all unrighteousness."

God is faithful.

Comfort, O Comfort My People

What a privilege for Isaiah to be called by God to comfort His people, especially after he had announced God's displeasure and forthcoming judgments. Chapter 40 begins a new segment in Isaiah, in which the Father takes Israel in His everlasting arms, drawing them close so they can feel the beat of His heart.

DAY ONE

As we begin our new segment of Isaiah, we'll find some new key words that we'll add to our bookmark. Today you'll read Isaiah 40, marking the key words already on your bookmark. Also mark *comfort,* references to the *coming of the Lord,* and *wait,*[35] and add them to your bookmark.

Why does Israel need comfort? What will bring comfort? What did you learn about God in this chapter?

Read the following verses and compare them to Isaiah 40:3-6. What do you learn?

Malachi 3:1; 4:5-6

Matthew 3:1-3

Mark 1:1-3

Luke 3:4-6

John 1:23

Record a theme for Isaiah 40 on ISAIAH AT A GLANCE.

DAY TWO

Today read Isaiah 41, marking the key words from your bookmark. Mark *servant* and note who the servant is and what you learn about him. Add *servant* to your bookmark. You began by marking *redeemed* in chapter 35. Now you can begin marking *Redeemer* the same way.

Redeemer is the translation of the Hebrew word that means the closest blood relative, who is obligated to redeem a family name, a heritage, and land. If a person or his land (his family's inheritance forever as God commanded) is sold to pay debt, the redeemer buys back the person, freeing him from slavery.

As you read through Isaiah 41, think through the content paragraph by paragraph. Seeing the flow of thought is important. Look for what is happening, what God is doing. How does the chapter start? What do you learn from the contrast between those who make idols and the servant?

What will God do for Israel? (Hint: Watch for the "I will" statements.)

Record a theme for Isaiah 41 on ISAIAH AT A GLANCE.

DAY THREE

The more you read Isaiah, linger in its message, and meditate on its precepts, the better you will understand God and

His purpose for having you study this book at this time in your life.

Read Isaiah 42 today, marking the key words from your bookmark. Mark *justice*[36] and add it to your bookmark.

You should have marked *servant* as you read. Is the servant in chapter 42 the one that's in chapter 41? How do you know? What did you learn about the servant in chapter 42?

What did you learn about God and the contrast between Him and idols?

Record a theme for Isaiah 42 on ISAIAH AT A GLANCE.

DAY FOUR

Read Isaiah 43, marking key words from your bookmark as usual. Also mark *Savior* (*saved, salvation*) and add these to your bookmark.

List what you learned about God from this chapter.

Notice also that the Chaldeans or Babylonians are mentioned. You've seen them before, in chapters 13, 14, 21 and 39. What did you learn here about them?

Record a theme for Isaiah 43 on ISAIAH AT A GLANCE.

DAY FIVE

Today's assignment is Isaiah 44. As usual, as you read, mark the key words from your bookmark. Note how Isaiah 44 connects with Isaiah 43.

Who is speaking in this chapter, and what did you learn about Him? What is the essence of His message?

What subject is dealt with in verses 9-20? Did you learn anything new about idols in this chapter?

Read 1 Corinthians 8:4-6 and Colossians 3:5. What insights into idolatry did you get?

Now read Exodus 20:1-6 and Deuteronomy 28. What did you learn about God?

What did you learn from Isaiah 44 about Israel as God's servant, and about God's relationship to Israel?

Who is mentioned by name at the end of the chapter? What is the future of Israel?

Record a theme for Isaiah 44 on ISAIAH AT A GLANCE.

DAY SIX

You observed five chapters this week, and it's time to pull it all together with some good questions for application. Remember that although Isaiah's message was to Israel, it has application today. Some of the application is for Israel, but the things we learn about God and His ways are also instructive for us. So let's dig in and worship God as we recount and relate His glorious ways today.

First, review what you learned about God, and then think about your life, your beliefs, your standards. How do they measure up to the Word of God? Do you view the world through the lens of God's Word or through the world's beliefs and philosophies?

Second, consider what you learned about Israel's future. What does this mean to you as a child of God?

Third, think about how Israel treated God. Have you ever had a child or loved one treat you the way Israel treated the Lord? Or do you have a friend who experienced this and shared it with you?

Have you ever done anything like this to God?

What have you learned this week about God and His

response to His chosen people when they do not honor Him as God?

Do you need to talk to God about anything in your life?

DAY SEVEN

 Store in your heart: Isaiah 40:1

Read and discuss: Isaiah 40–44

QUESTIONS FOR DISCUSSION OR INDIVIDUAL STUDY

- Discuss what you learned about God.

- What did you learn about your life as you reflected on how it measured up to the Word of God?

- Do you view the world through the lens of God's Word or through the world's beliefs and philosophies?

- Considering what you learned about Israel's future, how do you relate? What does this mean to you as a child of God?

- Has one of your children or a loved one ever treated you the way Israel treated the Lord according to these chapters? Or do you have a friend who experienced this and shared it with you? Discuss how it felt to you.

- Have you ever done anything like this to God? What do you think God our Father's reaction is when someone treats Him this way?

- What have you learned this week about God and His response to His chosen people when they do not honor Him as God?

Thought for the Week

This segment of Isaiah begins with the words, "'Comfort, O comfort My people,' says your God." This directive is given to Isaiah the prophet. "My people" refers to Israel, God's chosen people. As Isaiah writes this, he says that this directive to him comes from "your God," so he means that *Israel's* God has given him the ministry of comfort to Israel. The message from chapters 40–66 of Isaiah is about redemption and restoration.

If you're a Christian, you're one of God's people in a different sense. According to 1 Peter 2:10, those who have believed are the people of God. Gentiles (people from nations other than Israel) can become people of God by believing the gospel of Jesus Christ.

So how do you apply the message "'Comfort, O comfort, My people,' says your God"? Since the God of Israel is your God if you're a Christian, what does it mean to you to comfort God's people?

If we take "My people" as the nation of Israel, should we minister comfort to Israel? If we take "My people" in the New Testament sense of the church, should we minister comfort to the church?

"Israel" in Isaiah is the people of God, not the modern political state of Israel, which includes non-Jews as citizens. Furthermore, the modern state does not even include all of the Jews. Only about half of the Jews in the world are citizens of the modern state of Israel. So what can we do? How can Christians comfort God's people, Israel?

The first and most important way is to share the gospel. The gospel is universal. All have sinned and come short of the glory of God, Jew and Gentile. The wages of sin is death, and all have sinned, so all need salvation. The way of salvation for Jew and Gentile is the same—faith in the gospel of

Jesus Christ. Belief in the death, burial, and resurrection of Jesus, the Son of God, who made atonement for all sin by shedding His blood on the cross, is the one and only way to redemption, to salvation. When Isaiah speaks of redemption for Israel, he is pointing forward to these truths. Jesus is the light of the world, appointed to bring prisoners from the dungeon and to open blind eyes.

The second way to comfort Israel is to intercede on their behalf. We can intercede for Israel in prayer, and we can intercede in the affairs of men. The classic modern example of interceding in the affairs of men on behalf of Jews was the protection many believers extended to Jews during the Holocaust.

Another way to comfort God's people is to understand the ministry of comfort God gives us:

> Blessed be the God and Father of our Lord Jesus Christ, the Father of mercies and God of all comfort, who comforts us in all our affliction so that we will be able to comfort those who are in any affliction with the comfort with which we ourselves are comforted by God. For just as the sufferings of Christ are ours in abundance, so also our comfort is abundant through Christ. But if we are afflicted, it is for your comfort and salvation; or if we are comforted, it is for your comfort, which is effective in the patient enduring of the same sufferings which we also suffer (2 Corinthians 1:3-6).

This passage includes several points. First, we are to comfort as we have been comforted by God, the God of all comfort. Second, our comfort is abundant through Christ. Third, that comfort is to help us deal with our afflictions, our sufferings.

In other words, God comforts us so we can comfort others. This comfort is not the comfort of the world, but the comfort of God. Only those who know God's comfort can extend God's comfort.

It's important for us to understand comfort. The Greek word translated in these verses is the same one used in Acts 9:31 when the church was continuing to increase as it was "going on in the fear of the Lord and in the comfort of the Holy Spirit." And it is related to the word Jesus used when He said He will give His disciples "another Helper" to be with them forever, the Spirit of truth, the Holy Spirit (John 14:16). The Greek word translated *helper* there means advocate or comforter.

The Holy Spirit is our comforter. We operate in the comfort of the Holy Spirit, who indwells us and empowers us to live in obedience to God's commandments. The Holy Spirit stays with us until Jesus returns. God, the Holy Spirit, is always with us to comfort us and to empower us to comfort the church.

We comfort those not in the church, Jews or Gentiles, by helping them believe the gospel so their enmity with God can turn to peace. Once they find peace with God, they find comfort in the Holy Spirit, who is given to all who believe.

" 'Comfort, O comfort My people,' says your God."

I Am the Lord, and There Is No Other

∿∿∿∿

The nations worship idols made with their hands from pieces of wood, stone, or metal. God, however, is the creator of wood, stone, and metal. When you compare God to these false gods, you find many other differences. Idols don't speak, and idols can't save. Idols don't control the future. There is no one like God.

∿∿
DAY ONE

Before looking at Isaiah 45 today, reread Isaiah 44:24-28. What character has been introduced? Mark references to him, but don't add this to your bookmark. What does God say he will do?

Now read Isaiah 45 and mark the key words from your bookmark. Also mark the phrase *there is none else* and similar phrases such as *there is no other*. Add these to your bookmark. Also mark references to *Cyrus*.

Add to your list of things God says Cyrus will do and what God will do for him.

This prophecy regarding Cyrus was given about 150 years

in advance of its fulfillment. In 539 BC, Cyrus and Darius of the Medo-Persian Empire conquered Babylon. Read Ezra 1:1-11 and 2 Chronicles 36:22-23 to see the fulfillment of the prophecy in Isaiah 45.

What did you learn about God in Isaiah 45?

Record a theme for Isaiah 45 on ISAIAH AT A GLANCE.

DAY TWO

Read Isaiah 46 today, marking key words and phrases from your bookmark.

List what you learned about God and about idols.

What did you learn about Israel's future?

Record a theme for Isaiah 46 on ISAIAH AT A GLANCE.

DAY THREE

Read Isaiah 47 today and mark the key words and phrases from your bookmark. (*Chaldeans* is a synonym for *Babylonians.*)

List what you learn about Babylon.

Suppose you lived in Isaiah's day and heard this message from the mouth of God's prophet. How would such information possibly benefit you as an Israelite?

Record a theme for Isaiah 47 on ISAIAH AT A GLANCE.

DAY FOUR

Read Isaiah 48 and mark the key words and phrases.

Although Babylon is mentioned, it is not the focus of this chapter. Watch for references to time.

Summarize what you observed about Jacob (Israel).

What did you learn about the Lord, the Redeemer, the Holy One of Israel.

What did you learn from the last line of verse 16?

Record a theme for Isaiah 48 on ISAIAH AT A GLANCE.

DAYS FIVE & SIX

Observe Isaiah 49, marking key words and phrases from your bookmark.

Now, move carefully through the text, one paragraph at a time, watching who is speaking or who is being spoken about.

Who is the servant in verses 5-7? Who is the despised one?

Who are "those who are bound" according to verse 9—the *they, them,* and *these* of verses 9-12? What is the message in these verses?

Who converses in verses 14-21? Summarize what each person is saying.

What is God going to do according to verses 22-23?

What is the message in verses 24-26?

Record a theme for Isaiah 49 on ISAIAH AT A GLANCE.

DAY SEVEN

 Store in your heart: Isaiah 45:6-7

Read and discuss: Isaiah 45–49

QUESTIONS FOR DISCUSSION OR INDIVIDUAL STUDY

- ∾ Discuss your insights about Cyrus.

- ∾ What did you learn about Babylon?

- ∾ What is the future of Israel?

- ∾ Discuss what you learned about God and His interactions with Cyrus, Babylon, and Israel.

- ∾ Have you ever felt like Zion in Isaiah 49:14—that the Lord has forsaken you? What truths from these chapters help you counter the fiery darts of the enemy?

- ∾ What application can you make to your life from the principles in these chapters?

THOUGHT FOR THE WEEK

Some people say there is no god, but the psalms teach us that these people are fools. The wicked man says in his heart that there is no god, but that's just to justify his wickedness. Both fools and wicked people will meet surprise judgments.

Others think there are many gods, fashioning idols from wood, stone, or metal to represent them. Still others think they can become gods themselves. All these people craft a god to fit their own ideas. If the world knew the true God, they would know how futile their ideas are.

The Lord said, "There is none else, no other God" (Isaiah 45:14). Who is He, and what is He like? Why is it so hard for people to take God's Word at face value? He has told man about Himself throughout Isaiah. In Isaiah 40:18-20 and 44:10-19, Isaiah exposes the folly of those who make idols.

We might be tempted to laugh at the foolishness of such a

person. But we have to ask ourselves if we aren't guilty of the same thing in other ways. We don't bow down, but maybe we still worship such things.

What takes first place in your life? Some say, "My children!" Others might say, "My job!" If you had to place three things in priority, what would take first place? Oh, it's easy to give the "Christian" answer: "God, family, work." But is that how we live? At least the fool, with his little wooden statue that he carved out of the same tree he uses for firewood, has clear priorities. By bowing down before that block of wood, he shows what he places first.

We don't physically bow much at all in today's Western cultures. We might do it at some point in a weekly church service, but chances are we haven't bowed much more than our head. Kneeling is prominent in some worship services, but not all. And falling prostrate? Not seen much these days. We wouldn't want to make a scene!

And maybe that's okay. We certainly don't want to make a show of our holiness. However, how do we show submission to the authority of God? How do we "bow" to Him in submission? Do our lives reflect the priority we say we place on Him? Are Bible reading and prayer priorities for us? How else do we hear from God? How do we talk with Him?

That's one of the key distinguishing things about God. He hears. He sees. He talks. Here's what the psalmist wrote:

> Their idols are silver and gold,
> The work of man's hands.
>
> They have mouths, but they cannot speak;
> They have eyes, but they cannot see;
>
> They have ears, but they cannot hear;
> They have noses, but they cannot smell;
>
> They have hands, but they cannot feel;

> They have feet, but they cannot walk;
> They cannot make a sound with their throat.
>
> Those who make them will become like them,
> Everyone who trusts in them (Psalm 115:4-8).

The great contrast between idols that represent the gods man invents and the God of the Bible is that God is living. He sees what we do, He hears our cries to Him, and He speaks to us in His Word. Our prayers come up to Him as incense.

No one can make such a God in his mind or with his hands. God reveals who He is to us, and He demands that we bow down to Him in worship and submission. And He hears our cries and speaks to us words of comfort, as He did in Isaiah's day.

WHO HAS BELIEVED OUR REPORT?

∽∽∽∽∽

What do you know about Jesus? What do you believe? Have you got it right? It is truly a matter of life and death.

∽∽∽
DAY ONE

Read Isaiah 50 today, marking key words and phrases from your bookmark. Mark *ransom* the same way you marked *redeem*. As you read and mark verses 4-9, read carefully to identify the speaker.

Read the following verses and record your insights:

Mark 14:53-65

Matthew 26:59-67

Luke 22:63-65

What is God saying in Isaiah 50:1-3? What kind of answer does He expect to His questions? How do these verses relate to verses 4-9?

What is God saying about *light* in verses 10-11?

Record a theme for Isaiah 50 on ISAIAH AT A GLANCE.

DAY TWO

Read Isaiah 51, marking key words and phrases from your bookmark, and add any new ones you see in this chapter.

Whom is God speaking to in verses 1-11? What is coming, whom (or how far) will it reach, and how long will it last?

Why does the Lord tell His people to "look to Abraham"?

According to this chapter, how should you answer the question, "Who are you that you are afraid of man who dies?" (verse 12). Why should you answer that way?

Record a theme for Isaiah 51 on ISAIAH AT A GLANCE.

DAY THREE

Read Isaiah 52:1-12, marking key words as usual. We'll cover verses 13-15 with chapter 53 tomorrow.

Read Romans 10:1-15, watching for references to *salvation, righteousness,* and *believing (faith)*. Now note how the Spirit of God ties Romans 10:15 with Isaiah 52:7.

What brings salvation? What brings righteousness? How is a person made righteous? What is the relationship between salvation and righteousness?

Record a theme for Isaiah 52 on ISAIAH AT A GLANCE.

DAY FOUR

Today we'll cover one of the most important prophecies in the Old Testament. Read Isaiah 52:13–53:12. Before you mark anything, think about who the Servant is, based on the description. Who is He? Now read through these verses again, marking or color-coding as usual.

Read Mark 15 and Psalm 22:1-21. What do you see?

Also read Hebrews 1:3-4 and Philippians 2:5-11. What do you see about Jesus here that compares with Isaiah 52:13?

DAY FIVE

We're going to continue cross-referencing Isaiah 53 today so you don't miss any of the vital truths of this powerful chapter. Read through Isaiah 52:13–53:12 again and then compare these verses:

Isaiah 52:15 with Romans 15:15-21

Isaiah 53:4 with Matthew 8:14-17

Isaiah 53:5 with 1 Peter 2:24

Isaiah 53:6 (and verses 5,8,11,12) with 2 Corinthians 5:21

Isaiah 53:7-8 with Acts 8:26-40

Isaiah 53:8 with Daniel 9:26

Isaiah 53:9 with 1 Peter 2:22 (and remember what you read in Mark 15)

Isaiah 53:12 with Luke 22:37 (and remember what you read in Mark 15)

How vital is the message of Isaiah 52:13–53:12?

Record a theme for Isaiah 53 on ISAIAH AT A GLANCE.

DAY SIX

For our last chapter of the week, read Isaiah 54, marking key words and phrases from your bookmark.

Who is to be joyful and why?

What do you learn about God and His lovingkindness?

Determine a theme for chapter 54 on ISAIAH AT A GLANCE.

DAY SEVEN

 Store in your heart: Isaiah 53:5

Read and discuss: Isaiah 50:4-9; 52:13–53:12; 54

QUESTIONS FOR DISCUSSION OR INDIVIDUAL STUDY

- Discuss your insights from Isaiah 50:4-9 and Isaiah 52:13–53:12. Refer to the notes you made about the cross-reference. Take your time and discuss this thoroughly.

- What is the importance of these truths?

- How vital is it that people believe this message?

- How important is it to *you* to believe this message?

- If there's time, discuss the other chapters from this week's lesson. What is there to rejoice about?

- What is the proper relationship between the redeemed and man who dies? Between the redeemed and the Redeemer?

∾ What is your relationship to Isaiah 52:7? What should it be?

∾ What application can you make to your life this week?

THOUGHT FOR THE WEEK

The angel declared to the shepherds in the fields around Bethlehem that there was good news of great joy for all the peoples. What was that good news? A Savior.

Most people don't really get the idea of a Savior. If they did, there would be many more Christians in the world today. I'm reminded of a young woman with whom I had a conversation recently. "Saved from what?" was her question. You see, despite church attendance, she didn't understand the basic truths of these chapters of Isaiah or of many other passages of the Bible.

She didn't understand that we are all sinners (Romans 3:23). And sin separates us from God (Isaiah 59:2), putting us at enmity with God so that we don't have peace with Him (Romans 5:1), even if we're not aware of it. And sin has a price. The wages of sin is death (Romans 6:23). So we need someone, something that will remove the barrier, remove the enmity, and give us peace with God so that we are relieved of the penalty of sin, which is death. That someone, that something, is a Savior.

Now, who or what can be that Savior? First, the Savior needed to be flesh and blood so that through death and resurrection, He could defeat death. He needed to die, to shed blood as a sacrificial lamb. Second, the Savior needed to be sinless so that He would not be under the sentence of death, so that He would not have earned the wages of sin. Sin has spread to all mankind through Adam, the first man, and death through sin, so this sinless one could not be descended from Adam. So the Savior must be a sinless sacrifice, perfect and unblemished. He must be human and yet not descended from Adam.

The solution? God Himself would provide the sacrifice. He gave His Son, Jesus, who became flesh and lived among us (John 1:14; 3:16). Jesus was born of a virgin, Mary, so He did not inherit the stain of sin from Adam (no man was His father). He is God, so He committed no sin. In His sacrifice, however, Jesus would taste suffering as well as death. The Gospels record that suffering, and Isaiah prophesied it.

He was despised and forsaken by men, with many sorrows and grief. He was oppressed and afflicted, yet He did not open His mouth in reply. He was taken like a lamb to slaughter. He was crucified with two wicked men, yet a rich man, Joseph of Arimathea, provided a grave for Him. All these things tie Isaiah and the four Gospels together.

But the most important and most radical of the ties between the Gospels and Isaiah is this—He was pierced for our transgressions, crushed for our iniquities, and by His scourging we are healed. He bore the sin of many and interceded for the transgressors. Instead of you and me dying for our sins, He died. That was His intercession: *Righteous Judge (God the Father), don't punish them with death for their sins, punish Me. I'll take on their flesh; I'll take on their sins; I'll die in their place.*

And that substitutionary sacrifice, that atonement for sin, that propitiation or satisfaction of debt was accepted by the Father, who healed us of our transgressions. The chastening for our well-being fell upon Him instead of us. All that Jesus did in His death, the Father accepted as full payment for what we owed. By His scourging we are healed.

But that's not the end of the good news. It doesn't stop with mercy, by us not receiving what we were due. God's grace in this matter extends beyond mercy to the gift of eternal life. Through Jesus' resurrection from the dead, we also have resurrection to new life, to eternal life. We may die physically, but we have eternal life with God, and our ultimate end state with God in the new heavens and earth will include no more death, no more crying, no more mourning, no more pain.

Everything prophesied in Isaiah about Jesus was true—even going back to Isaiah 7:14, where we saw a virgin would be with child, whose name would be Immanuel, God with us. This child from Galilee, from the town of Nazareth, on whose shoulders the government would rest—He would be the Wonderful Counselor, Mighty God, Eternal Father, Prince of Peace. He would bring peace on earth, peace with God, peace for you and me and all who would believe in His death, burial, and resurrection. This is Jesus, the Son of God, the Lamb of God.

We are saved from sin's penalty by a Savior, God Himself. But we're also saved from sin's power by God Himself. After Isaiah, other prophets—Jeremiah, Ezekiel, and Joel—prophesied of the Spirit being poured out on those who believed. This is God the Holy Spirit, sent by Jesus to be a Comforter, a Helper. The Holy Spirit indwells all who believe (1 Thessalonians 4:8) and seals us in Christ (Ephesians 1:13) as a pledge of our inheritance.

The Holy Spirit is the power God promises (in Ezekiel 36:26-27) to enable us to obey Him and resist sin. In other words, those who are saved from the penalty of sin are also saved from the power of sin. We do not have to sin because we have the power in God the Holy Spirit living in us to help us choose to obey. The devil doesn't make me sin, and the Holy Spirit doesn't make me obey. But I'm no longer powerless—sin doesn't control me. I can grow in obedience and in godliness.

So we're saved from sin's penalty and sin's power. But

what else? We will also be saved from sin's presence. Not in this life, in this mortal body, but in the next. First Corinthians 15:50-55 explains that we must have an immortal, imperishable body to inherit the kingdom of God. We will no longer have a body that has inherited sin from Adam, so we will be free from sin. In the new heaven and earth, there is no more death, for our mortal bodies will be replaced by new ones that will be immortal and imperishable.

Saved from sin—its penalty, power, and presence. By a Savior, God's Son, who took on flesh, took on our sin, and paid the price of death for us so we can be healed of our transgressions. We need a Savior. The good news is that we have one—Jesus.

DOES GOD HEAR OUR PRAYERS?

❧❧❧❧

God invites us to come to Him. He invites us to seek Him, but He sets the conditions. He invites us to call upon Him. But He only listens when we ask in the right way, with the right motives. What are we to do? We must know His Word, believe it is true, and live by its truth.

DAY ONE

Read Isaiah 55 and 56 through to get the flow of thought. Then mark Isaiah 55 with the key words and phrases from your bookmark. We'll tackle Isaiah 56 tomorrow.

Now, what is the invitation, and what is the basis of the invitation—the reasoning or appeal? To whom is the invitation given, and what is the benefit of responding?

Read Revelation 22:17 and compare the invitations.

In Isaiah 55, what is offered to the wicked and why? What do you learn about God?

Record a theme for Isaiah 55 on ISAIAH AT A GLANCE.

DAY TWO

Read Isaiah 56 today, marking key words and phrases. Mark *house of prayer* as you do *prayer*.

What groups are addressed in this chapter, and what is God's word to each?

What do you learn about the house of prayer? Why do you think it is called this and not *house of sacrifice*? Read 2 Chronicles 6:19-21,32-33,36-40; 7:12-16.

Record a theme for Isaiah 56 on ISAIAH AT A GLANCE.

DAY THREE

Before tackling Isaiah 57, start reading from Isaiah 56:9 and continue through the end of Isaiah 57 to see the flow of thought. Now read Isaiah 57 again, marking key words and phrases from your bookmark as usual. Mark, but don't add to your bookmark, the phrase *I will heal him*. Watch especially for contrasts.

How does Isaiah 57 relate to Isaiah 56? What is contrasted in Isaiah 57?

Read the following and summarize what you learn about peace:

Isaiah 9:6-7

Isaiah 26:3,12

Isaiah 32:17

Isaiah 48:22

Isaiah 52:7

Isaiah 54:10

Isaiah 55:12

Isaiah 57:2,19,21

What would you tell someone who was looking for peace?

Record a theme for Isaiah 57 on ISAIAH AT A GLANCE.

DAY FOUR

Isaiah 58 is the longest passage about fasting in the Bible. As you observe it, mark references to *fasting, light,* and *darkness* in distinctive ways. Add *light* and *darkness* to your bookmark.

List what you learn about the fasting Israel was doing. What was right or wrong about it?

Look for cause-effect relationships—because this, then what? What is the result of the right kind of fast or right attitude of your heart toward God?

Record a theme for Isaiah 58 on ISAIAH AT A GLANCE.

DAY FIVE

Read Isaiah 59 today, marking key words from your bookmark. Be sure to mark *light* and *darkness* again today. Also mark *truth.*

Now, what is Israel's problem? What are they doing? What has been God's response so far?

Read verses 15-21 again. What is the Lord's response to Israel's spiritual condition? The word *intercede* in verse 16 means to plead on behalf of someone, to mediate in a dispute.

Read Isaiah 59:1 again, and also read the following verses:

Proverbs 15:29

Proverbs 28:9,13-14

Psalm 6:8-9

John 9:31

1 John 1:9

What is the relationship between sin and prayer?

Read the following verses and summarize what you learn about the *covenant:*

Jeremiah 31:31-34

Jeremiah 32:36-44

Ezekiel 36:22-28

Ezekiel 39:21-29

Record a theme for Isaiah 59 on ISAIAH AT A GLANCE.

DAY SIX

Our last chapter for the week is Isaiah 60. Read the whole chapter, identifying who *you* refers to before you start marking. Then as usual, mark the key words and phrases from your bookmark.

What is the tone of this chapter? Compare Isaiah 60:1-3 with Isaiah 9:2; 42:6; and 49:6. Do you see any connections?

Now read Revelation 21:1–22:5 and compare what you learn about light with Isaiah 60:19-20. What are your insights?

Finally, record a theme for Isaiah 60 on ISAIAH AT A GLANCE.

DAY SEVEN

 Store in your heart: Isaiah 59:1-2
Read and discuss: Isaiah 55–60

QUESTIONS FOR DISCUSSION OR INDIVIDUAL STUDY

- ∽ Discuss the invitation God gives to the thirsty.

- ∽ What insights did you gain from your study of light and darkness?

- ∽ Discuss the covenant God makes with Israel. Does it apply to non-Israelites?

- ∽ How do the nations relate to Israel and God's promises?

- ∽ What do these chapters teach us about world peace?

- ∽ Discuss what you learned about fasting.

- ∽ What is the relationship between sin and prayer?

- ∽ How do these chapters bring comfort to God's people?

THOUGHT FOR THE WEEK

The Lord's ear is not so dull that it cannot hear, according to Isaiah 59:1. But God doesn't respond to our cries the way we expect if we don't ask with the right heart.

Isaiah 55 invites those who incline their ears to hear, to listen to what God is saying. Isn't it interesting that God asks *us* to listen, and often we don't? Then we ask *Him* to listen, and we think He doesn't hear us when He doesn't answer the way or when we want. What's the problem?

Isaiah 59 gives us part of the answer. We're asking with the wrong motive. That was the problem with the Israelites' fasting in chapter 58. Fasting was about seeking God, looking to Him, asking Him to help. But if our motivation for fasting is wrong, our fast might as well not even be happening. James taught the same thing about prayer:

> You lust and do not have; so you commit murder. You are envious and cannot obtain; so you fight and quarrel. You do not have because you do not ask. You ask and do not receive, because you ask with wrong motives, so that you may spend it on your pleasures (James 4:2-3).

It's not that God's ear is so dull that He *cannot* hear. We ask with wrong motives.

Israel was fasting for "contention and strife and to strike with a wicked fist" (Isaiah 58:4), thinking that would make their "voice heard on high." But they had the wrong motive, so God did not respond to what they asked. The same is true today, James says. Asking with wrong motives won't get you what you want.

Similarly, Isaiah 59:1-2 shows that our sin separates us from God. Proverbs and Psalms make it clear that God hears the prayers of the righteous, not of those who turn away from His Word and regard wickedness in their hearts. John wrote that God hears those who fear Him and do His will, and that if we confess our sins, He will forgive us our sins (John 9:31; 1 John 1:9).

The psalmist asked who could ascend to the holy hill of God:

> Who may ascend into the hill of the LORD?
> And who may stand in His holy place?

He who has clean hands and a pure heart,
Who has not lifted up his soul to falsehood
And has not sworn deceitfully.

He shall receive a blessing from the Lord
And righteousness from the God of his
      salvation (Psalm 24:3-5).

The prayer of the righteous man, offered in righteousness, with the right heart, is a pleasing aroma to God. And He hears our prayers. The psalmist pictured this—coming before the Lord with clean hands and a pure heart. First John 1:10 tells us that if we say we have not sinned, we make God a liar and His Word is not in us. So we still must confess our sin to approach God with clean hands and a pure heart so our prayers can be a sweet aroma before Him, pleasing Him. And then His face won't be hidden from us so that He does not hear.

The Lord Has Anointed Me to Bring Good News

∿∿∿∿

Jesus stood up in the synagogue in Nazareth and found the place in Isaiah we call chapter 61, verses 1 and 2. He read it aloud and then said, "Today this Scripture has been fulfilled in your hearing." These profound words declared that He, Jesus of Nazareth, was the fulfillment of the promise of Messiah.

DAY ONE

Today we begin our last week of study of this marvelous book of prophecy. We start with a thrilling quotation from Isaiah in Luke 4:16-21. Our remaining six chapters are filled with good news and quotable verses. We'll take them one at a time for six days. Savor them. Enjoy them as you linger over each verse and remember the promises from the previous 60 chapters.

Read Isaiah 61, marking key words and phrases from your bookmark as usual.

Now, in Luke 4, notice where Jesus stopped reading. Did

111

you see that He only quoted the first part of Isaiah 61:2? Only that much of the prophecy was fulfilled that day. What Jesus did not quote was not yet fulfilled.

Read the following, and then list what you learn about vengeance:

Isaiah 34:8

Isaiah 35:4

Isaiah 47:1-3

Isaiah 59:17-18

Now according to Isaiah 61, what comes *after* the day of vengeance? Read the following and compare what you learn:

Isaiah 42:11

Isaiah 44:23

Isaiah 49:13

Isaiah 51:3,11

Isaiah 54:1

Isaiah 55:12

Isaiah 65:13-14,18-19

Record a theme for Isaiah 61 on ISAIAH AT A GLANCE.

DAY TWO

Read Isaiah 62 through and identify whom the word *you* refers to. Now read and mark key words and phrases. Watch for references to time.

What is the promise for Jerusalem and for Israel?

Who are the watchmen in verse 6? How long are they to give the Lord no rest (verse 7)? How will they do it?

Record a theme for Isaiah 62 on ISAIAH AT A GLANCE.

DAY THREE

Read through Isaiah 63 before marking. You need to discern who is coming from Edom so you can mark references according to your pattern. Read Isaiah 59:16 and Revelation 14:14-20.

Bozrah was in Edom (now part of the modern country of Jordan). Edom is another name for Esau, Jacob's brother, because he was red. The mountains of Edom today are reddish. The ancient city of Petra, also in modern Jordan, is in the ancient territory of Edom.

Now read and mark Isaiah 63.

Compare Isaiah 63:1-6 with Isaiah 61:1-3. What connection can you make?

If you want to dig a little deeper and have the time, read the following:

Acts 1:6-12

Zechariah 14:1-17

Revelation 16:12-16

Revelation 19:11-21

Joel 3:9-17

When Jesus will come to fight for Jerusalem against the armies surrounding her, where will He come from? Is there any evidence of a battle at Megiddo (Har-magedon or Armageddon), or is the battle in Jerusalem, or is it farther south, in Edom? When Jesus stands on the Mount of Olives, has He come directly from heaven or somewhere else?

This is food for thought, Beloved. Some teach that Jesus will return to the same spot on the Mount of Olives based on Acts. Others say He comes in the *same way* He left. Have fun discussing this!

Finally, record a theme for Isaiah 63 on ISAIAH AT A GLANCE.

DAY FOUR

The final three chapters of Isaiah are just glorious. You might want to curl up in a quiet place and just drink in Isaiah 64–66, reading and reflecting without marking anything yet. Just see the magnificent flow.

Now read Isaiah 64 and mark as usual. Mark *come down* and *meet*[37] in the same way, but don't add them to your bookmark.

Now, what do you learn about God the Father? Anything that applies to you?

From verses 10-12, what has happened to Jerusalem and the temple? Isaiah wrote long before the Babylonians destroyed the city and temple. How do you understand these verses?

Record a theme for Isaiah 64 on ISAIAH AT A GLANCE.

DAY FIVE

Read Isaiah 65 to see who is speaking. Then read and mark the chapter. Mark references to the *new heavens* and *new earth*.

Compare verse 2 to Isaiah 1:1-4.

We've seen judgment for sin throughout Isaiah, especially chapters 1–39. We've also seen comfort and compassion, especially since chapter 40. How do you see these themes in chapter 65?

What distinction is made between God's servants and others? What are the consequences to forsaking the Lord?

Previously, we looked at people crying out to God and God either hearing or refusing to listen because of iniquity. What do you see at the end of chapter 65 that contrasts with that?

When will these events take place?

Record a theme for Isaiah 65 on ISAIAH AT A GLANCE.

DAY SIX

Finally, Beloved, our last chapter. On the one hand, it's exciting to get to the end of such a long book. On the other, it means that our time together in this glorious book has come to an end. But what a privilege it has been to explore Isaiah with you. I'm sure many verses will remain with you forever. And although we might not understand everything in Isaiah, we can stand firmly on those things we do understand, so rejoice.

Read Isaiah 66 and mark key words and phrases from your bookmark as you have done these 13 weeks. You should mark references to the *new heaven* and *new earth* as you did yesterday in Isaiah 65.

What did you learn about God? Isn't it glorious to think of who He is and what He has done? And don't you long to be one of those to whom God will look?

What do you learn about the future of Jerusalem? How does it relate to the nations and to you?

What do you learn about the Lord's coming and about the new heavens and earth?

Compare what you learn in Isaiah about the new heavens and earth with 2 Peter 3:13 and Revelation 21.

Compare what you learn from Isaiah 66:24 about the worm not dying and the fire not being quenched with the following, and then note your conclusions:

> Mark 9:42-48
>
> Matthew 3:11-12
>
> Matthew 13:36-43
>
> Matthew 18:8
>
> Matthew 25:31-46
>
> Jude 7
>
> Revelation 19:19-22; 20:11-15; 21:8

The difference between the lake of fire for unbelievers and the peaceful repose of those who have believed the gospel should move each of us to share the truth. How did this study affect you?

Finally, record a theme for Isaiah 66 on ISAIAH AT A GLANCE.

DAY SEVEN

 Store in your heart: Isaiah 61:1-2

Read and discuss: Isaiah 61–66

QUESTIONS FOR DISCUSSION OR INDIVIDUAL STUDY

∽ Discuss all you've learned about the coming of the

Lord—His first and second comings. What are the differences?

∾ What is the future of Jerusalem? Ultimately, what will Jerusalem be like?

∾ How will the nations relate to Jerusalem and Israel in the end?

∾ What did you learn about God in these chapters that will provoke you to change the way you live? What will you share with others?

∾ Discuss the new heavens and new earth, and the lake of fire.

∾ What project will your group take on to help mankind know the truth of Isaiah? Be creative and practical, but concrete—something you can and will do. How will you share the good news?

THOUGHT FOR THE WEEK

In the Revelation of Jesus Christ communicated by His angel to His bondservant John, John saw a new heaven and a new earth, for the first heaven and the first earth passed away. It is "the new Jerusalem, which comes down out of heaven," in which there was no temple, "for the Lord God the Almighty and the Lamb are its temple," and there was "no need of the sun or of the moon to shine on it, for the glory of God has illumined it, and its lamp is the Lamb. The nations will walk by its light, and the kings of the earth will bring their glory into it." In it there is no curse, no death, no mourning, no crying, and no pain.

Oh, what a glorious day that will be! But what comes before that day, and what do we do in the meantime? What did we learn in the final chapters of Isaiah, in *all* of Isaiah?

First, sin must be judged. We know from Isaiah that the first coming of Jesus pays the price for sin. His resurrection from death confirms our resurrection and assures us that death will not hold final power over us though we die here on earth in our mortal bodies. His first coming assures release from captivity—freedom to those who were prisoners of Satan and of death.

But Jesus' second coming also brings the day of vengeance of our God. The penalty of sin is paid for by Jesus' crucifixion, but those who do not believe the gospel must still suffer judgment for sin. All those who reject the Word of God, the gospel of Jesus Christ, must bear the consequences of their unbelief. This is the just judgment of the just and holy God of the universe, creator of all that dwells on the earth, in the sea, and in the heavens. He who is pure truth, pure holiness, all-powerful and all-knowing, will not let those who do not believe escape. Justice demands it. Love demands it. Mercy merely delays it until all grace is given toward mankind and the earth in which he dwells.

So we look to the future and see a duality that is real and true, sure and fair, decreed from the beginning, and inevitable to the end. God judges sin and gives comfort to those who believe Him. God uses whatever instruments are needed to accomplish His purposes. He brings glory to Himself through many means. One is by being faithful to His Word. He does what He promises.

He promised a land to Israel as an inheritance forever. He promised to restore Israel from being trodden down, persecuted, and attacked by the nations. He promised to send a Deliverer, a Redeemer, a Savior. He promised to do this Himself for the people He chose as His own, the Israelites, the land He chose as His own, Israel, and the city He chose to place His name in forever, Jerusalem.

He promised Adam and Eve a seed who would crush

the serpent. He gave us Jesus, conceived by the Holy Spirit in the virgin Mary so that He was without sin and could pay the price of a perfect ransom, His blood unstained by sin. He promised a seed to Abraham who would bless all mankind. He gave us Jesus, descended from Abraham. He promised a descendant to David to sit on His throne forever. He gave us Jesus, descended from David. He promised the people who walked in darkness a great light, from Galilee of the Gentiles. He gave us Jesus of Nazareth, the Light of the World. He promised a Wonderful Counselor, Mighty God, Eternal Father, Prince of Peace, and He gave us Jesus, His Son.

"For God so loved the world that He gave His only begotten Son that whoever believes in Him shall not perish, but have eternal life" (John 3:16).

Isaiah lived in the days of Uzziah, Jotham, Ahaz, and Hezekiah, kings of Judah, more than 2700 years ago. His message to these kings and Israel in those days was a message of hope that despite the danger from nations around them, despite the sin among them, despite the righteous judgment of God upon sin and sinners, there was hope. God Himself would redeem them. He Himself would make the way for them to be restored to the place He had originally designed for them.

So it is with us, Beloved. We who are Gentiles, not of Israel, not Jews, have the same redemption from slavery to sin, the same inclusion in God's family, the same inheritance of riches as joint heirs with God's only begotten Son, Jesus. We face the same judgment for sin, but we also face the same hope, the comfort, the promise of a new heaven and a new earth, a new Jerusalem, a new creation in which none of the consequences of Adam's sin attach to any part of creation.

All creation groans, longing for this redemption from corruption to freedom in Christ, according to Romans 8. Do you? Do you long for that promised future? Do you long for all those you know to have the same redemption? What about those you don't know? Do you long for them to escape the destruction and judgment that is certain to come upon them, if not in this life then in the next?

What will you do about it? Will you just read Isaiah, and be glad for its message? Or will you take the message of Isaiah and make it your mission? Billions of souls depend upon watchmen to warn them of danger coming. Ezekiel teaches that if you sound the warning trumpet and you are ignored, you are not guilty of their blood if they die in their sins. But if you do not sound the trumpet and they die in their sins, you are guilty of their blood because you did not warn them.

Isaiah warned the people in his day. And God appointed watchmen not only to warn the people but also to give Him no rest until He establishes and makes Jerusalem a praise on the earth (Isaiah 62:6).

If you accept the appointment of watchman, you have two tasks. First, warn people of the danger coming, of the sword that will sweep them away in judgment if they do not believe the gospel of Jesus Christ. Second, storm the gates of heaven in prayer that God will come down and meet us—in judgment on sin and in redemption for mankind. Pray fervently for Jesus' coming, that righteousness might abound on the earth and that the day of the new heaven and new earth might soon come. Come quickly, Lord Jesus!

SEGMENT DIVISIONS

				CHAPTER THEMES
	DISCOURSES REGARDING JERUSALEM	GOD'S CHARACTER AND JUDGMENT	1	The sad truth about the nation
			2	The day of judgment
			3	
			4	Promises
			5	Judgments + blessings
			6	Isaiah's assignment (response to being forgiven)
			7	Misplaced trust in Assyria vs God
			8	
			9	
			10	
			11	
			12	
	ORACLES		13	
			14	
			15	
			16	
			17	
			18	
			19	
			20	
			21	
			22	
			23	
	DISCOURSES REGARDING THAT DAY		24	
			25	
			26	
			27	
	WOES		28	
			29	
			30	
			31	
			32	
			33	

SEGMENT DIVISIONS

			CHAPTER THEMES
	GOD'S RANSOM	GOD'S CHARACTER AND JUDGMENT	34
			35
	HISTORICAL INTERLUDE		36
			37
			38
			39
	DISCOURSES REGARDING:	GOD'S COMFORT AND REDEMPTION	40
			41
			42
			43
			44
			45
			46
			47
			48
	DISCOURSES REGARDING:		49
			50
			51
			52
			53
			54
			55
			56
			57
	DISCOURSES REGARDING:		58
			59
			60
			61
			62
			63
			64
			65
			66

THE RULERS AND PROPHETS OF ISAIAH'S TIME

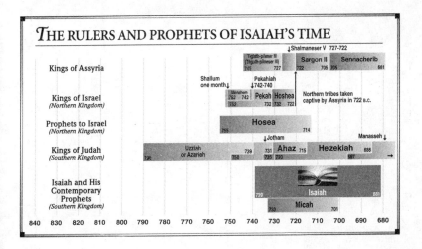

THE NATIONS THAT RECEIVED THE ORACLES

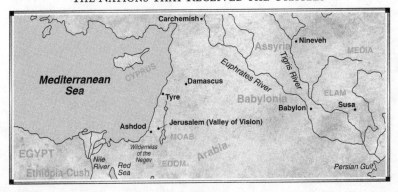

NOTES

1. KJV, NKJV: lofty; NIV: arrogance; ESV: haughty
2. KJV, NKJV, ESV: bow down
3. KJV, NKJV: captivity
4. KJV, NKJV, ESV: conceive
5. NIV: nations
6. ESV: Ah
7. NIV, ESV: survivors
8. KJV, NKJV: consume (consumption)
9. KJV, NKJV: rod
10. KJV, NKJV, NIV, ESV: in that day
11. NIV: all the lands
12. KJV, NKJV: hell; NIV: the grave
13. NIV: LORD Almighty
14. KJV: howl
15. KJV: spoiler; NKJV: devastation
16. NIV: so
17. KJV, NKJV: counsel
18. NIV: planned
19. KJV, NKJV, ESV: terrible; NIV: terror
20. NIV, ESV: traitor betrays
21. KJV, NKJV: fashioned
22. KJV, NKJV, ESV: mourning
23. KJV, NKJV, NIV, ESV: look(ed) to
24. KJV, NKJV: rejoice; NIV: reveling
25. KJV, NKJV, ESV: purposed
26. KJV, NKJV: just
27. NIV: (NIV doesn't translate knowledge—mark teach)
28. KJV: hearken; NIV: pay attention; ESV: give attention
29. KJV, NKJV, ESV: fight; NIV: do battle
30. KJV: vile person
31. KJV: churl; NKJV: miser, schemer; NIV, ESV: scoundrel
32. KJV: liberal; NKJV: generous
33. KJV: Idumea
34. KJV, NIV, ESV: way
35. NIV: hope
36. KJV: judgment
37. NIV: come to the help

$\mathcal{D}$o you want a life that thrives?

Wherever you are on your spiritual journey, there is a way to discover Truth for yourself so you can find the abundant life in Christ.

Kay Arthur and Pete De Lacy invite you to join them on the ultimate journey. Learn to live life God's way by knowing Him through His Word.

Visit www.precept.org/thrives to take the next step by downloading a free study tool.

Books in the
New Inductive Study Series

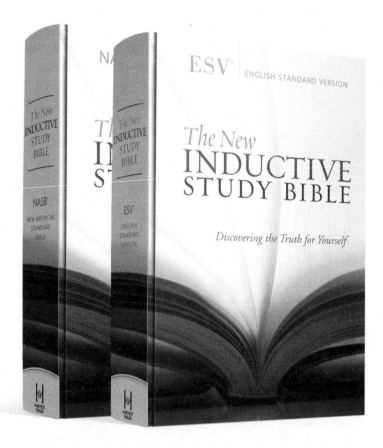